Phil Mclean grew up in the industrial north east of England. He grew up in an extended family of love, independent thinking, school boy dreams and distant or bureaucracy and pollution.

He originally planned to study commercial art. Yet inspired by his uncle, he changed career objectives to food and hospitality.

Self-determination and the dream of greater opportunity saw the travel to Australia in 1969. He has had a successful career in retailing, holding various senior appointments with major brands.

Now retired, he lives on the north coast of NSW with Katie.

To Ethel Higginbotham to whom I owe so much.

Phil Mclean

DEATH BY DEMENTIA

Test of Love, Loyalty and Passion

AUSTIN MACAULEY PUBLISHERS™

LONDON * CAMBRIDGE * NEW YORK * SHARJAH

Copyright © Phil Mclean 2022

The right of Phil Mclean to be identified as author of this work has been asserted by the author in accordance with section 77 and 78 of the Copyright, Designs and Patents Act 1988.

All rights reserved. No part of this publication may be reproduced, stored in a retrieval system, or transmitted in any form or by any means, electronic, mechanical, photocopying, recording, or otherwise, without the prior permission of the publishers.

Any person who commits any unauthorised act in relation to this publication may be liable to criminal prosecution and civil claims for damages.

All of the events in this memoir are true to the best of author's memory. The views expressed in this memoir are solely those of the author.

A CIP catalogue record for this title is available from the British Library.

ISBN 9781398433793 (Paperback)
ISBN 9781398433809 (Hardback)
ISBN 9781398433823 (ePub e-book)
ISBN 9781398433816 (Audiobook)

www.austinmacauley.com

First Published 2022
Austin Macauley Publishers Ltd®
1 Canada Square
Canary Wharf
London
E14 5AA

My sincere thanks to the volunteers at the Tea Gardens Community Technology Centre who patiently worked through my 'at times indecipherable writings' thereby creating a suitable document ready for consideration by a literary agent.

And to Katie, the focus of this little story. As usual, her patience with me as I explained how I was going to create a 'Best Seller' for Dementia support.

Tables of Contents

Thoughts of a lifetime	11
1) Barnabas, Bereavement and Beer – A Polluted Life	13
2) Observations of a Scatter Brain: College, Canada, Louise Zoo's and Kangaroos	44
3) Commitment, Coles and Kentucky	77
4) A Caravan Park, Alcoholic's Amyloids, Carcinoids and Charity	94
5) Incompetence, Incontinence and a Royal Commission Showcase	111
6) The China Challenge, Tangles and a Potentially Terminal Affair	129
7) Drugs, Mental Health, Communication and Conclusion. Bureaucracy Killing Democracy	162
Key Words	179
Appendix	180

Thoughts of a lifetime

- Paul Marshal. My dearest childhood friend. We should have gone into business: painting, decorating or bodybuilding.
- Iris Hall. I hope you found lasting love and loyalty. You are a true Lady.
- John Fordham Jnr. She really was a beauty when finished, a Bluewater pocket rocket.
- Colin Scott-Smith. I often wonder if you still eat herrings in tomato sauce with marmalade.
- Colonel Harland Sanders. You taught me what racism looked like in America. Regrettably still extremely evident today.
- Tony Deluca. The most honest and honourable public servant that I worked with.
- Kevin Davies. A great boss and a lovely human being.
- Peter Walkley. An inspiration, tremendous company and you gave a pommy English boy his first job.
- Chris Scorgie. A dear friend, who I failed when you needed support. I am extremely sorry.
- CJC. One of the greatest influences in my life. Says little, suggests a lot.
- Graham Reynolds. You should have lived by the same standards you expected of others.
- Frank Fisher. The King of Tonga is still the best story in my repertoire.
- Gordon Spence. Was becoming an African Mercenary such a good idea, considering the alternative – a British officer's pension.
- Tom Tomlinson. Many have walked in your shadow; few have achieved the respect.
- Jim Adolf. Thank heavens that the string never broke. Your favourite Channel 7 boss would have been devastated.

- Dad. You taught me trust and independence – even if I was a little late in the expectation.
- Aunt Nan. Dreams and imagination – anything is possible, you just have to believe.
- Grandmother. Never let me down. Tough love and I never got to pay back my dues.
- Uncle Jack. Would have loved Australia. Bush skills, adventure, exploration and fishing.

1) Barnabas, Bereavement and Beer – A Polluted Life

Hi

My name is Phil (Philip to my Grandmother and older family). I am 71 and I have cancer. The technical dialogue is Neuroendocrine Tumours or put simply: a carcinoid and metastatic, just adding to the fun, my wife Katie is 74 and has Alzheimer's. This is our story. A test of love, loyalty, passion, pollution, politics, patience, incontinence and incompetence. Death by Dementia.

I was born in 1948, October 11th to be precise. Philip Charles McLean, registered at Stockton-On-Tee's (The Steel River – Chris Rea), to Charles Harold McLean, Master Hairdresser and Olwen McLean nee Allan, Hairdresser. Both were previously married, having lost respective partners during WWII. Fathers first wife to a small bomb, galloping consumption, and mother's husband to a very raucous bomb, German in origin, with no personal intention or consideration.

Stockton-On-Tee's evolved as a significant participant in the planets first trial and the creation of pollution, identified as capitalism and consumption, played out as the first Industrial Revolution of the 19th century. Adam Smith's "Wealth of Nations" set the scene. Colonisation, power and greed-the establishment at play. Bridges, trains and ships. Steel monsters bellowing soot and debris with no consideration nor identity to the future health of humans and the planet. The grand years of prosperity were a mere memory, however, the remnants of a once-mighty Empire still obvious by the decaying empty buildings. A brief reprieve created by a futile war effort whereby the once "Britannia Ruled the Waves", had won the war, consequently losing the peace. The spirit was damaged – not broken. War brought them together as a community – indecision and politicians split them apart soon after.

Grey and green could best describe the weather and seasons offering in the North East of England. However, during the short warmer green respite periods, smog was ever present. Ruddy brown roofs of pollutant fallout from the once world's largest steel foundries of Dorman Long (builder of the Harbour Bridge in Sydney Australia) and the Billingham Petro/Chemical Behemoth of ICI. Acrid cloud was a daily ritual, dependent upon wind velocity and direction.

Excuse me, I just hear Katie getting up. I have to help with her morning activities. The ever-changing compendium of Alzheimer's reaction. This morning she has soiled her incontinence pants, stained the bed which will need changing and another wash load of goods. Showered and the mess re-sanitised and we are ready to dress, clean the teeth with the ever expectation of breakfast. No thanks, just the reality of this oft-daily routine of slow decline.

Where was I? Yes, pollution. The River Tees and its great historical past. My mother did not know at the time; she had contracted Tuberculosis (TB) during the latter part of the war. Working in a munitions' factory, supporting the war effort justifiably spending many nights in air raid shelters, a less splendid residence of squalor: if a bomb didn't get you, the disease generally did.

We initially lived in my mother's house from her first marriage within a suburb of the greater region – Thornaby. My father and mother opened a hairdressing salon on the main road in a shopping precinct of Middlesbrough. Life was full of hope and wants. Those that had 'money' wanted luxuries of life, cast aside during the war. The salon and its offering quickly gained a reputation, a crèche was contemplated and "pretty bottles" of body lotion and hair tonics were my mother's intention. As our income climbed, more staff were trained and "Charles", the name of the business, grew into a highly successful income-producing entity. Life was full of rejuvenation and enjoyment.

As the bank account increased, my mother's health deteriorated and, optimistic to the end, my father sought the very latest in medical opportunity. Life for me was wonderful. I was both loved and spoilt, Little Lord Fauntleroy. Visits to various specialists around the country were an adventure and an education. Staying at the Savoy Hotel in London at five years of age, table manners and etiquette was a must, and experimentation with taste. Frog legs and escargot, caviar and canapés. All offered for experience and choices of life's food bowl.

Uxbridge, the centre of spitfire warfare during the war. Now full of hope, growth and 'Biggles'. My Uncle Paddy, Air force ace to the core and I think that the plane was a spitfire two-seater trainer. To a young boy, his first flight was everything. So, with my father beckoning me on like a skilled pilot himself, I took to the grey skies over Uxbridge with Uncle Paddy. Memories of the war ever-present, daily thoughts of many good friends who never "won that fight" but not spoken of with show-merely sadness.

An innocent boy with comic book concepts, questioning the action of relativity, and the answers coming back after all those years, forming what I have become. How one behaves, how to treat others, treading gently. That ego breeds conceit and conceit manifests in arrogance. That war is the greatest failure of the human species, specifically politicians by namesake.

"What was it like Uncle, the war?"

"Something that I hope that you will never have to experience Philip."

"Were, you scared?"

"Of course, Philip, everyone was scared, however your survival instinct surfaces. You have to concentrate, focus on the job at hand and do your best. You have to believe in something, someone, and you need luck, lots of it, it's not a game, and it's the real thing."

More 'joy' flights followed, many questions always answered, never referred to as 'me' always a 'we'. Looking back, the emphasis was always that, as an individual, you must try your hardest (to live in Uncle Paddy's circumstances) to survive. However, adopt a 'we' (team mentality). I am saddened today looking at, for example, our team sports. How many promote through social media, 'individuality', 'look at me, aren't I wonderful'? Sadly, not so in many instances. Inappropriate role models for young people who adopt the wrong traits of weaker, not strong character practice. The herd mentality.

As my father's wallet fattened so, my mother's body frame thinned. The TB had now created two major operations and most of her time was spent in bed. My grandmother started to visit, then staying – ultimately playing the daily preparatory role in my life. Ensuring I always had healthy breakfast, shower and clean clothes prior to school. Grandmother was not stern, however, quite often serious and I found myself being questioned as to certain activities that she may not approve of. To my mother I was an angel, to my grandmother I was a spoilt child who had to become independent. Strong headwinds were on the horizon and she knew that I had to be better prepared.

So, the wet shoes and socks that were thrown into the bedroom (after wading through the creek, catching frogs on the way home from school) had to be put in front of the fire to dry. We had since moved from our house in Thornaby to a new suburb 'in the country' at Brookfield Gardens. Surrounded by farms, paddocks, horses and creeks. It was a child's playground. Meant to create 'cleaner air' for my mother, we nonetheless could still see the constant pollutant cloud from Dorman Long and ICI. However, I am sure that the moving idea was naively well-intentioned. I had to help peel potatoes and prepare items for dinner – I was given chores, and I did them. Lunch or dinner, always a ritual, generally roast meat and two vegetables, roast potatoes and the best gravy any mortal has ever tasted to this day, followed by a home-cooked sweet pie, custard and water. No Coca Cola in this household. Maybe lemonade for Sunday lunch.

When my father arrived home, dinner was always eaten at the table; mother would initially join us, although later, more and more dinner was served to her 'in bed', on a hospital-style trolley table. After dinner, I initially got (had) to dry the dishes and put them away. Gradually gravitating to, wash and dry, always a communal affair and never left until later. It was then outside: feed the hamster and play with the rabbit and dog (which spent most of her time at the end of mother's bed). Then it was, "Go and get washed and get into your pyjamas and don't forget to clean your teeth." Wouldn't our young children of today be better prepared for life's future trials if they all had this routine? Simple non-harming personal discipline. Respect for self, person and property. We certainly may have less dental issues – irrespective of Coca Cola addiction. I would then talk to mum and be off to bed.

Life was quite normal for a boy growing up in the '50s. Cowboys and Indians, your first chemistry set and the usual tricks, 'generally on an irate grandmother who couldn't see the funny side'. Catching tiddlers and frogs in the local stream, always out in the fresh air, wet socks more often than not and invariably returning home with a stray dog in tow. "No, you can't keep it, Philip, it belongs to Sam and Judy in No. 26 and you know that!"

About that time in my youth, my mother's health must have deteriorated further, as she was taken to hospital and stayed some weeks. I visited twice with my father and I don't think that he was sure what to do. Let a seven-year-old see the reality of the impending death of a mother or shield him from the agony. I would often go to my Nana's on a Sunday, something I did not particularly enjoy and, I realise now, it was my father's desire that I keep interacting with my mother's mother.

We had a bathroom, a shower and a 'normal flush toilet'. Nana didn't. Bath night was a large metal tub pulled into the kitchen where it was filled from the copper and I was duly 'bathed'. The toilet was outside in the backyard in a dedicated structure. Known as a pan. You did your thing into a receptacle that was removed and replaced weekly. No toilet paper at Nana's, just cut-up newspaper. She did not have a television and the house was always freezing cold. Oh yes, and dinner: boiled egg, toast and rice pudding. No roasts here.

I suggested to father that if I had to stay with Nana, I would possibly perish from malnutrition. I recollect the comment was, "They had to raise three girls and one boy on a very limited income during the depression, as such old habits and frugality are hard to forget. You should be grateful for what you have; many are less fortunate. Pride comes before a fall son, remember that." I certainly didn't get it.

My father was extremely busy, business was booming and his skills as a hairdresser had spread far and wide. His enthusiasm and attention never waned, whilst of course, I realised later his life was hell. The realisation that whatever you did, your wife was going to die. The second one to boot.

He decided that to be closer to my mother he would buy a suitable premise that could house both the business and home. So, after extensive renovations (it had been a plumber's workshop on the ground floor with two levels of living above), we all moved to 88 St. Barnabas Road, Middlesbrough, a few streets away from the Middlesbrough football club, relatively close to the old salon on Linthorpe Road, plenty of parking and public transport. Grandmother suggested that her son had her in mind when purchasing. An older person's home adjacent (she called it the workhouse, a dim reminder from the turn of the century), major Tees-side hospital and morgue. Monumental stonemason on the corner adjacent and cemetery at the end of St Barnabas road! She had a vibrant wicked sense of humour.

The salon was exclusively modern by the then standards, with pink and black décor, and reception area at the front, waiting area and to the rear, the hair salon a room to the left housed washing machines and a huge dryer for the mountains of black towels. To the rear outside the backyard was an aviary with a multitude of exotic birds, a customer toilet to the side and finally a workshop and garage.

Upstairs was the main bedroom and dining room to the front and rear bedroom (mine) then lounge, kitchen, bathroom and pantry. Up another flight of stairs was another bedroom and a small box room. Intercom connected mother from the bedroom to the salon providing a constant stream of friends and customers to sit and talk to her.

Grandmother, who was not getting younger, had time to go to her home for periods and my father was able to take care of the daily needs, which he did excellently. I was able to 'get away with far more than the old chilly bottom', my, at that point in time, nickname for grandmother, given her maiden name was Higginbotham. Get the point.

However, Barony's Road held little for a young boy. No longer the fields, streams, paddocks, horses and cows. Just row upon row of terrace style soot-covered homes, shops and once more quite obvious pollutants, cars, buses and trains. I hated it. So, holidays and weekends it was off to Aunt Nan's (Nancy, Dad's sister) and Uncle Jack. Holiday periods were spent in various parts of the country, however with one favoured destination – Whitby. Fresh air, the ocean, boats, fishing (smoked Haddock commonly coined as Whitby Kippers, the best on the planet). Camping and walking. No iPhone here. Just more wet socks and stray dogs.

Time spent with the horses. Aunt Nellie and Uncle Vic's daughter Margaret, who had her own horse. As such, I was given riding lessons at the Toc H stables, Acklam. Nellie and Vic were not real aunt and uncle, merely good family friends.

Aunt Nan and Uncle had a lease Cafe in Barnard Castle, the building was a historic landmark with a dungeon (inclusive of 16th-century armour). Cromwell had stayed there. This involved hours of fun with Cousin Greg, dressing in somewhat large 'beast plates, helmets and such'. The swords were about the length of our bodies.

It was after one such outing that I was taken back to Aunt Nellie's and Uncle Vic's. I remember that when I entered the hall to the lounge, that the house was unusually dark, indeed all the curtains were drawn. It was around 2:00 pm and that day there was no smell of roast cooking for dinner, no table set and no radio noise. Just my father sitting in Uncle Vic's favourite chair. I instinctively knew something was dreadfully wrong and he calmly told me that my mother had died. He told me that she loved me immensely and was now 'out of pain and at peace'. The rest of the day was, still is a blur, where I spent most of the time in my bedroom crying.

For the next few days, I stayed with Aunt and Uncle, whilst dad presumably took care of the arrangements with the rest of the family. I was not asked to go to the funeral nor was I taken to see her. I didn't ask and it was not offered. To this day, I have shied away from funerals. The only ones who attended, being my father, Win and a friend's mother.

So that first chapter of my life was over, I was nine years of age and nothing would be the same again. Having lived to this stage of my life with my mother in bed almost continually, it had been seen as the norm with the expectation that it would go on forever.

I had not really understood how the circumstance had affected my father, both in the long period of mother's health, the highs and lows of the illness, for which at that point no cure was available, and the final loss.

On our travels, whether staying with relatives, friends, hotels or just going for a drive with mom, dad would always stop and 'have a pint or two'. I had never seen him drunk; he never ever swore (except bugger) and if he had ever been tipsy, he was always a 'happy person'. I never (ever) saw him angry with anyone. Annoyed yes, angry no. However, he would debate and articulate any point of conversation or a particular topic that he felt passionate about. He was a Freemason, attending the lodge on the allocated evening, and he also went to a club, which was mainly of returned servicemen. I remember he was quite proficient at snooker. He never ever gambled that I was aware of. However, after my mother's death, he would spend longer in the club or pub and I saw less of him during the school week, annoying Gran immensely if he was late for dinner.

Grandmother took care of my daily needs. Berated me regularly about my lack of interest in school study, always insisting how Chris (Christopher) and Gregory (Greg) were doing so well. I lost interest, missed my mother incredibly and hid my tears. The next few years were a blur, I sat my II plus, an exam that dictated your future direction in the search for a job or career. A good result and you went to Grammar School with the future expectation of university. A lesser grade and you were placed in a school that taught more practical than academic skills. The understanding that you would become: a plumber, electrician, boilermaker, fitter and turner and the like, an honourable trade.

Whilst to this day many theorists disagree with this particular exam in the belief that you were categorised for life – 'marking you in a class of possible inferiority', I feel that it nonetheless created an outlet for those that may not do well in exams or excel in maths or English. As such, trades – a significant debate within the industry. Those possibly lost to the job market versus international trade work visa introduction, due to trade skill shortage in specific regions. I believe today that if we had this sort of vocational schooling, we may not have youth lost to the system of gainful employment, instead of bringing in overseas trade skills to fill the gap. Tafe is not the answer, children, and young minds; need to start developing practical aptitude at an earlier age. For Philip Charles McLean – 6th generation Charles, it was Whinney Banks Boys School (no girls shock horror), teachers that we called "Masters" and we were McLean, Spence, Marshal. Only in the last year did anyone call you by your Christian name and that was only a few of the more skilled masters. However, whilst one could only describe me as a somewhat disruptive know it all, pain in the backside pupil, the masters were excellent. The only problem being that I paid little attention to what they were trying to impart. Mostly in their 30's and 40's they had recently seen and participated in WWII. They were, therefore, in many aspects older and wiser for the experience. The one subject that I both seriously enjoyed and excelled in was art. Most of my education years saw me at the top of the A form for art. I am not a very proficient abstract thinker so my works centred on still life, body form, horses and calligraphy. Geography was fun because we explored the aspects of topography and basic forms of determining how to read maps and indeed test our survival team skills in excursions to the North York Moors. More importantly, Mr Gaskell, the Geography Master, had only one leg, thereby becoming a point of caricature discussion for that particular subject matter. Not that he ever discussed how the leg became disengaged from the body; we learnt that from P.E. Ball (the gym instructor) that Mr Gaskell had been in the Atlantic war convoys as an engineer. A U-boat put pay to his ship and he was taken prisoner and sent to a P.O.W. camp. Having escaped and finding his way back to the UK, he re-joined another ship. This time he was 'not so lucky' losing his leg in a ships attack, this time hospitalised to a P.O.W. facility. Quite some man. What a great shame that some of our teaching profession to date, without wartime culture, do not have life's skills and the subsequent positive input, specifically how to handle male youth testosterone and stupidity.

Quite incredible, as with Uncle Paddy (Air force), my father (Army), Uncle Jack (Army) Middle East Campaign and Uncle Vic, Indian Regiment British Army.

Not one mention of the war and none of these men, looking back, were in any way 'damaged' or suffered from any stress-related issues. They did all smoke, some quite heavily, however, that would seem a small price to pay for the ordeals some experienced. They were all happy persons, somewhat insular at times, but no melodrama or discussion of war, no Facebook, no glory-seeking, principally revered by all. How sad that attitude did not transcend to Vietnam, another failure of bureaucracy and insult. The medals of WWII, some WWI, left in the cupboard – the future was their family. The only discussion I ever heard was both the respect for Churchill and the disdain for Chamberlain, quoted as a weak public servant who had no feelings for human nature, misreading or ignoring the obvious and that which Hitler was clearly planning. A man that had no 'ticker' and should have never been allowed to hold that position in the office. That Churchill should have been listened to too sooner. We will never know as it certainly happened, and as today, our politicians never learn, read history or both. The wrong persons, in the wrong position of responsibility for the wrong reasons. My terminology – control freaks.

School days I found boring, I was not interested in sport (unless it was a swim period) or long-distance running, both of which I was quite capable of. I paid little attention to lessons with declining grades in English, Maths, Geography, History and Science and PE. Always top of the A form for Art.

My father bought me a pony, Brandy, and we stable, agisted her behind the Bluebell Hotel, close to our old home at Brookfield Gardens and the hotel conveniently positioned as a favourite venue of fathers. There was a tack room, dressage ring and jumps set up in the rear paddock. So, when nights permitted and invariably weekends, I spent my time grooming, platting, cleaning saddles and tack.

Margaret agisted her horse there and was now highly proficient at show jumping. I was keen to learn more; regrettably, Brandy seemed to develop a quite typical McLean trait, stubbornness. We would confidently head for the bars, the ditch, the drum configuration and all would be well for a time, suddenly (I must have been dumb or something) the ears would go back and she would stop dead in her tracks. I invariably ended up on the ground, bruised but not defeated. So, any thought of a career with horses quickly disappeared, not with that horse anyway.

My father decided that I needed to do some form of menial tasks during school holidays/long weekends, so I was enrolled into the salon on Barnys Roads after school and Northallerton Saturday mornings. I swept floors, washed down basins, filled bottles, sterilised scissors and combs and eventually 'snuggled' up to wealthy customers. Lady Siller or Mrs Winterschladen always gave tremendous tips much to the annoyance of the girls styling hair. Again, I became an older Little Lord Fauntleroy, Charles' son and heir, Charles Jnr. maybe Charles II, or so my father thought. Or possibly, I was to become the second Mr Charles, Mr Philip.

It was during this period that I, only once, received what was termed a 'clip around the ear' justifiably so. Dennis, dad's business partner left early, and dad was left to cash up. We were therefore later than normal, paying little attention to the sound of screeching tyres in the marketplace outside. My father locked the doors and we headed for the car. Unfortunately, stolen. Consequently, after the police reports were completed, we headed to the pub until friends arrived to take us home.

Months later, Dad was invited to the police stolen goods facility to identify his car, I went for the ride. All we were shown was a range of 'stock cars'. Dirt track racers that were built with bull and roll bars given the nature of the racing spectacle, and with no identification marks (all removed) it was impossible for my father to say which one, indeed, if any was his vehicle. Enter detective McLean Jnr. "Can I look inside Dad? I can tell which one is ours."

"How could you tell son?"

"Inside Dad."

"Okay, have a look. Is that alright Sergeant if my son looks inside the cars?"

"Yes, that's fine." A mark nine Jaguar vintage had a mahogany dashboard. Remember, boys have penknives. Penknives are adept at carving initials discreetly. PCM. 1959. I finally found our car. Yes, you have it; my only ever 'clip around the ear'.

School continued in its recurring boring nature, however, one day a revelation occurred. Mr Benbow the Science Master suggested to the Head, Mr Reid that he wanted to take a group of boys to Ostend/Rotterdam. We had encountered many excursions locally; however, to go overseas was something else. There was a particular group of boys, Marshal, Oakley, Bainbridge, Spence and Robinson and of course myself and with others. The excursion was organised. We were allowed to wear casual clothes, long pants and one suitcase each. A coach to Dover, ferry to Calais and so the adventure began. I saw our Masters in a different light, more relaxed, less formal and we had group discussions focused on what we did outside of school, and what we wished to pursue after school completion. This ultimately progressed to individual discussions about school attitude, results and improvement.

Other than Spence and I wreaking havoc on a couple of go-karts, the trip was focused on war history and which still remained as a stark reminder of what had occurred 16 years before. Specifically, the D-Day landings and senseless loss of life, how Churchill had not wanted to take 'his boys in'. The Americans of course did and they still are! Museums, art galleries and places of cultural significance and more discussion as to our respective future opportunities. The outcome being a commitment to study, initially for our Northern Counties School Certificate.

Marshal wanted to become a mechanic, Bainbridge a secondary school teacher, Oakley an electrical engineer, Spence a fighter pilot (he was already in the Air Traffic Corp. and held a junior provisional licence). Robinson my memory forgets and McLean a commercial artist.

Back at school, all seemed forgotten about our commitment to Mr Benbow and Mr Thomas. The routine of buffoonery reigned until one day Mr Ball told me that Mr Gaskell wanted to see me after the English lesson. That could mean only one thing, the cane. A small group had recently 'snuck' into the girl's school gym rooms, pinching some knickers and bras from the lockers, justifiably hauling the collection up their quadrangle flagpole. Hilarious, but Mr Gaskell did not see the joke and of course, I refused to 'dob in' my small group of merry renegades.

The cane followed, he was an expert at 'nicking' the end of the fingers and whilst it hurt, in reality only one's pride and it certainly never killed anybody. Then came an impassioned conversation that, in my situation, I actually had the capacity (I recall the word brain used frequently), if I focused, studied hard and actually applied myself for a short period of my life, I might even do well at school. Mr Gaskell started to spend more time working with me on both Geography, English and a chosen subject, Commerce. This subject was optional for the Northern Counties exam and it inspired my desire to one day earn a lot of money. At that point not appreciating how that was to happen. Whilst wishing to earn pocket money, dad secured a job during the holidays for myself and Cousin Chris. The facility, if I recollect, was some form of small engineering foundry on the outskirts of Stockton.

Chris was my idol, intelligent, articulate, excelling in sport and destined for creativeness, everything that I was not. His mother (Aunt Pat was dad's youngest sister) and Uncle George. They decided to migrate to Canada with baby cousin

Jennifer looking for better opportunities whilst at the same time seeking a better education for their son, boarding at a school, just outside Barnard Castle.

Consequently, most holidays were spent with the Bakes (Aunt Nan and Uncle Jack) and, during the course of our youth, many tales could be told recalling camping and hiking etc. around many destinations: Whitby, the Lakes District or Scotland. The mode of transport was a Bedford van into which we would pile the necessary camping, fishing and comfort items for pristine living at various camps sites. To this end, I idolised Chris as more the older brother and mentor than a cousin. He would discuss Dickens, Shakespeare, Huxley, and Fitzgerald to name a few and undoubtedly was instrumental in my later studying for my GCE O-levels, some years later.

The foundry work continued during school holidays and this was a period during which, I only ever saw my father use force to subdue a situation that he found intolerable. He had been a 'bare-knuckle' boxer in his teens fighting in an area of ill repute called Tillery. The pub there, now the Stockton and Thornaby Masonic Lodge, had been a haven for criminals, vagabonds and the like at the turn of the 19th century, whilst the tall ships still traversed the Tee's. Later, he joined a boxing group fighting welterweight and winning. Photos of the day show a young version, quite thin, of a Clarke Gable image. He had been extremely fit and myself even at 16 years old and Dad, now in the early 1960s, overweight, a heavy smoker and extremely unfit. However, I could punch him as hard as my strength would allow, in the stomach, and he never flinched. Back to the story, I was starting. At the bus stop, with a group of "working ladies" from the factory next door waiting for the bus. A man (extremely drunk) was blaspheming 'c' and 'f's' – flowing freely. In my upbringing this was unheard of, indeed, I at around 12 or 13 years old, had rarely ever heard those words, only from men working in the foundry. I realised later that this was the old man's way of 'toughening me up' and preparing me for the different classes of an individual. Suddenly and expectantly, the Jaguar pulled into view and dad got out. Usual attire, double-breasted suit and bow tie. "Hello son, I'm going over to your grandmother, do you want to come?" At that point, the drunk started his foul raucous tirade. The old man walked over, said excuse me ladies and said to the drunk, "You have had a little too much to drink and I do not think it appropriate to use that form of language specifically not in front of these ladies. At best it's men's front bar talk."

The drunk let loose at my father as to "who the xyz did he think he was, the great F-ing Charles?"

Dad just calmly once more said, "Look, I have asked you nicely to respect these ladies; I will not ask you again." The drunk uttered but two profanities and in a split second, my father let loose with first a left hook followed by a right and the drunk went down like a sack of potatoes.

What followed was, "I suggest you go home and sober up," to which the drunk replied, "Jesus Charles, they said you used to be very good, they weren't kidding, I'm sorry." Shocking you say! Today my father would be charged with aggravated assault locked up and the key thrown away. For what, standing up for a group of harmless defenceless women? Believing it was wrong to use foul language when the English language is quite beautiful if learnt and used correctly. All the man had was a sore nose, chin and a bruised ego. I'm with my father not the Chamberlains of this world.

In Adelaide, South Australia in the 1960s a young lawyer, Don Dunstan was trying to forge a career in politics. He ultimately became a successful social reforming Labour Premier in 1976. Yes in '76, he banned plastic bags from supermarkets. It was 2017 for NSW before someone had the guts to follow, dreadful. He introduced waste, can and bottle recycling which dramatically transformed the scape of South Australia. Ultimately making it a leader in the introduction of clean waste, and other options – wind, solar and battery power.

What has this got to do with my father's incident? The foul language, street drunkenness and potential street violence, not to mention worker abuse and respect for others in Australia? Weak political culture. Inappropriate legislation and the containment of "animalistic tribal behaviours" by humans changed to "freedom of right", everything is on the table.

Don was bi-sexual (in those days a closet homosexual for fear of imprisonment given that homosexuality was a criminal offence). As his career progressed, he moved to change what was known as the Lotteries Act, in specific terms, Section 63 which referred to loitering of individuals in common areas. His objective, in simple terms, was to remove the applicable section that would eventually make homosexuality a non-criminal offence for consenting adults. A worthy cause and long overdue. However, he was constantly advised that to change this section would have future implications for society, which may mean changes in behaviour that could have intentioned consequences to both society and individuals. Various Attorney Generals advised their concerns. However, hell-bent on creating 'equality for his kind' he ignored the warnings over the years, therefore not ensuring change that would protect aspects of the act, whilst establishing equality for homosexuality. In the redrafted format, drunken behaviour, both inside and outside premises proliferated. Foul language became too much the norm. 'Pommy bastard' once an Australian form of endearment was replaced with 'fuck' as though a part of normal discussion and behaviour. Street violence ensued, foul language and of course domestic violence became the accepted way of life and Australian society and politicians accepted the erosion of virtue, self-respect and educational standards, shrouded in the belief that this form of activity was acceptable. We are certainly paying the price now – the failed disciplinary requirements, education outcomes and mental health attributes.

I digress.

The foundry was followed by farm work, Egton Bridge, North York Moors. Farmers George and Andy Moore. I learnt how to milk a cow, a goat, how to store potatoes and turnips for winter use and how to deliver a calf. The importance of "mucking out" and rudimentary driving of a tractor, followed by sorties up into the paddocks in the old Land Rover. I loved it. Fresh eggs, thick cream and Andy's freshly baked bread. Real milk, straight from the cow. Rabbit, and the subsequent casserole, trapped by George and I in strategically positioned traps. The rabbit, not the casserole, Andy cooked that! Dad would pick me up on a Sunday afternoon and with George and Andy following in the old Land Rover. We would stop at the Egton Bridge pub for beer, or three – a lemonade and bag of chips for me, on the way home and back to Whinney Banks School, pollution, exams, trapped in this suburban bleak jungle of terrace houses, fish and chip shops, and crazy football fanatics.

If Middlesbrough Football Club were playing a home game, the surrounding streets would be full of cars and it became my job and my next-door neighbour, Alan Gill to look after them. This meant apprehending the unsuspecting driver whilst parking the vehicle, that 'for sixpence mister', we would watch that no one touched the vehicle whilst the game was on. This income-producing venture was carried out with swift efficiency as Alan and I walked each side of Latham

Road as more vehicles parked for sixpence. This was the start of motor vehicle purchase for the masses, replacing a pushbike – therefore highly treasured and as such a good opportunity for budding security agents. We also ensured that certain space allocation was left clear for neighbours returning from work. It worked well until Alan died.

We used to go 'bird watching/egg spotting' on the Gare. This was a manmade rock formation, a breakwater if you wish, that was a superb habit for watching and recording bird activity, egg counting, type of egg and bird etc. On a particular day, dressed in wet weather gear, I said goodbye to my father, "Where are you going?"

"To the Gare with Alan."

"No, you're not, the weather is too unpredictable, you could get washed off the rocks."

"I can swim, dad!"

"Don't be stupid and smart, you may be a good swimmer however, you are not going," and when he said no, that meant no. "I lost your mother and I don't intend to lose you," Alan went, was swept off the rocks and was found dead shortly after. It was an extremely sad time for a close-knit community, Alan was (or so we thought) the only child of Mr and Mrs Gill, corner shop owners and subsequently well known by the community.

Another testing time, although quite some years later, grandmother told me a story that impacted me for many years, indeed how I raised my own daughter. Mrs Gill apparently had a child out of wedlock, a terrible sin in the '40s. As a young girl, she was sent away to give birth and the child was adopted, never to be seen again. Consequently, over the years on visits back to 'Barny's Road', I visited Mr and Mrs Gill and it was extremely sad to see two people so lonely, having lost two children, however never spoken.

Years later when I met Katie, she already had a child, Louise, who was approximately 14 months old. Our relationship became serious and when we married in November 1970, the deal was this: no ifs or buts that Louise would be raised Catholic to satisfy her grandmother and family desires (I was atheist at the time) and, at a stage that I felt her mature enough I would tell her that I was not her biological father. Katie objected; a father had not been named on the birth certificate so Louise would never know. To me, that was morally wrong and was not going to happen, rightly or wrongly. I won the debate and subsequently told

Louise around 12 years of age. Then and indeed to this day Katie has only ever referred to him as 'Chick'.

Back to Whinney Banks Boys and I sat for my Northern Counties exam, I passed five subjects and Mr Gaskell said he was pleased; however, I could have done better and it was possible that I showed anxiety during 'the sitting for an exam'. At this point and I do not recollect the specific reason; however, I was packed off to Scotland. Aunt and Uncle Capalgill, an old lodge outside Moffet, Dumfries shire on the River Moffet, onto the Annan, then the ocean. A great salmon river where spawning took place up from 'the Grey Mares tail' into St Marys Loch. For anyone who has not seen a roe loaded fish fighting its way up from the ocean to the locks, it's one of the true wonders of nature. That this fish navigates its way back to where it was born, battling rocks, floods, leaping waterfalls is remarkable. Another wonderful area of exploration for a young restless boy.

Aunt and Uncle's business had been placed into bankruptcy in Stockton. Catering, kitchen design, supply and fit-out. I am not sure that Aunt knew the term 'owners' equity' or possibly more shoes. She was, God bless her, the original Imelda Marcos, without the nasties or arrogance. Uncle had studied commercial design and draughtsman drawing at Bradford. He was also incidentally, a brilliant drummer, having played in the forces whilst in the Middle East and, after demob, on vacation in Whitby. He was the drummer in the band playing at a hotel in Whitby when he met Aunt Nan, a very attractive woman of great wit, charm, spoke French and spent many hours singing to Edith Piaf. Grandmother, very protective of her two darling daughters was always critical of their partners. It was as though she didn't think them good enough. One particular discussion I remember was my father commenting jokingly, "She never liked any of them till they were dead."

Anyway, whatever Uncle Jack aspired to, they never had any money. Nan was forever borrowing money from grandmother, who always broke yet miraculously found £50, a sizeable amount in those days for her spendthrift daughter. And then there was dad, he was always a 'soft touch' ever protective of his sister, yet always complaining about her lifestyle. Aunt always had to buy "a new hat, handbag or shoes" and certainly had impeccable dress sense. Since youngster's, grandmother had always played a role in clothes and shoes that Chris or I would wear. It was generally a tailor and my first real suit was, however, a well-cut quality (greenish in colour) hand me down, an altered suit from Chris. He got the new one and after that, I now realise Aunt and Grandmother had a tremendous influence on me, how I later dressed and the quality hand-stitched suits that I gravitated to having moved from salmon to business stream.

Away from the grandmother, I now had to learn to iron. Greg was always fastidious with this ritual and it always annoyed the bejesus out of me, that if going out, we would always be waiting until he got that last minuscule crease out. I never did enjoy ironing however, it's one of life's many disciplines, and in so many situations, and one never appreciates when the exercise will be required. Your wife's dementia in question is a good start.

No TV, records, still vinyl were 33's – it was Piaf, Dorsey or Crupper. Greg had a wooden block on a snare drum stand and with that, he learnt to paradiddle, twirl and hit to the beat. He practised incessantly and became extremely proficient. Then, of course, it was 'come on Dad'. "Yes, come on Uncle, let's see you do it." Uncle would sit down and pick up the sticks. It was pure magic what he could do with such a basic sound shell. You start to realise that little is not less. Practice, determination and creativity can be achieved if someone wishes to put in the hard yards. I had not identified that theory at that point in my brief life.

For me, it was Moffat Academy, new teachers, new friends and a mixed school. Girls and that meant once more both an attraction, more importantly, distraction. Art came to the fore and I was soon 'top of the class' however, all other subjects were at the bottom. I remember little of that period of scholastic delay, not so the outdoors. Freedom to wander the burn, building dams, collecting wood, fishing in the Loch, and of course 'tickling' salmon. The basic principle, somewhat like horse whispering or as such, mesmerising the fish to come to you. This is how; you lay on the bank of the Burn, over an outcrop, under which the salmon will often rest on their travels back to the ocean. You place one hand, palm uppermost, under the ledge within the water. If you are in luck, a fish will meander over your hand and you gently extract the species out of the water. Easy, after a great deal of practice and patience. Salmon was around one pound Stirling per pound with a twenty-five-pound fine, if caught by the Bailiff.

On one particular day Greg and I when organising dinner, (they are particularly delicious cooked in a salmon poacher – no pun intended), realised that a bicycle heading in our direction, near a road overpass, was indeed the bailiff. Running like mad, we made the bridge overpass, sitting in fear underneath. The bailiff passed metres away not aware of two potential career criminals slipping from his grasp. What seemed like hours and we heard the sound of the Massey Ferguson tractor. Mr Murray, a local subsistence crofter who lived close by, and whose wife managed to feed four children on half a pound of mince and tatties (potatoes) as the luxury, and fish. An extremely meagre income, resilient, hardworking, generous, and happy. As father often said of specific types of person 'the salt of the earth son'. Mr Murray, to our surprise, stopped and the next thing we hear, "It's alright boys; you can come out now he has gone." Sheepishly we emerged, greeted by a hearty laugh and the request to see our catch. Of course, we had left the fish in the Burn in our panic – it was possibly halfway back to the ocean by now. He leant over to a lever on the tractor and lowered the bucket, wow! It was full of salmon! We had our poached salmon for dinner with little said.

Uncle Jack, whilst a very happy easy-going person, was best described as a 'bit of a loner'. He was extremely happy to sit all day, lost to his thoughts, fishing. He would go off on our camping excursions and sit for hours on his own, fishing. If extreme weather prevailed, his pipe and a few sips of green ginger wine warmed the soul. He was a tremendous role model for loyalty to one's family, independence and outdoor health pursuits. He was also extremely conscious of what one should eat, specifically that which was more appropriate to a healthy lifestyle. He was also an adaptive experimental cook; he made a mean Nettle soup, something that now attracts 'trend' attention 55 years later. He was very generous whilst extremely frugal: contented with less, yet happy if more was attained.

Not so Aunt Nan, extreme emotional energy, the life of the party, loved the high life, good food and drink, never stopped talking and looking back. Now possibly at the point, unfulfilled in potential career opportunity, Uncle had hitchhiked from Stockton to Moffat, then walked a not inconsiderable distance to the house. Completely broke financially, but not broken, after the failure of the catering business in Stockton. During that period, grandmother kept them financially afloat; otherwise, food would have been sparse. However, there was always laughter, light argument and generally as to something, that Greg or I had done that displeased. Yet again, I have no recollection of ever hearing any form of disagreement from aunt or uncle towards each other.

My father sent money for my board, anticipated for providing the food stocks, and cigarettes for my aunt. However, the visit to the food provider was always the same – a limited supply of food, the highest quality. It was to be the best cut of meat; exotic preserves, cheese, eggs, sour dough breads and fruits, generally not available in those days, now accepted 24/7. Maybe a bottle of Glen Fiddich if aunt could persuade uncle, although she always did.

We ate like gentry, for three to four days and then it was back to poached salmon, mince, tatties and uncles nettle soup. Cigarettes, in general, had no filters, and in desperation with much fun aimed critique, my aunt would keep the ends of the cigarette, and, when nothing else was available, the old tobacco was rolled in newspaper and smoked. This episode created merry discussion whilst, with hoots of laughter and comment. We passed judgement, "Yuk, aunt how could you" and "Mum that's disgusting" from Beth. We would sit around a roaring fire, being told dream stories and opportunities. Listening to Chevalier, Piaf or the like. Things improved, aunt got a job as a clerical/receptionist in a local hotel whilst uncle had found employment in a kitchen (commercial) design and installation organisation, a company he worked for until he finally retired as a director. I moved back to pollution, no burn, no salmon, just my 'O' levels.

There are periods reflected in my life where I have limited memory of what occurred. You will see this during my story and whilst I will deal with the topic in depth later, the apparent result of this "memory loss" was a severe blow to the head. In short, I was catapulted through the passenger side windscreen of a car when involved in a serious traffic accident. The driver of the other car died and I ended up in Teesside Hospital – 400 head stitches, a rebuilt nose (leg cartilage) and reaffixed left eyeball back into the socket. More lately, needless to say, memories can be lost through trauma. Memory confusion, not unlike dementia.

I have limited recollection of study; however, I passed my subjects, particularly enjoying the English language, English literature and History. Something that without doubt helped future career aspirations. My five GCE subjects plus Northern Counties and Art portfolio, enabled acceptance for art school at Leeds University. However, Uncle Jacks initial work history, design and our discussion must have registered the basic premise, being that there may be more opportunity in 'hospitality' for a more practical aptitude. Whether he thought my art was not good enough, or that, as it proved correct, hospitality helped me create choices in my future career that I could never have imagined. However, I soon found myself employed in my first full-time employment as a trainee manager at the Linthorpe Hotel. Owner: Les Walker, wealthy businessman, well acquainted with the who's who of business in the northeast of England.

The hotel would today be described as 'boutique'; it was an older pleasant looking building in quite spacious grounds, situated in a more affluent demographic suburb of the Greater Middlesbrough area – if that could be described as such. The hotel consisted of a 'working' men's bar/pool room at one end of the hotel. The riff-raff, out of sight, nonetheless I later came to realise, the income-producing area of significant importance to the overall profitability of the business. To the front was the reception, stairwell to upstairs hotel accommodation and extremely well-appointed flat (apartment) for Mr and Mrs Walker. To the left of the stairwell was the dining room (table d'hôte menu, lunch and dinner seven days and breakfast). Behind the door was the double entry to the commercial kitchen, larder and access to the cellar and cold room (not refrigerated). To the right of the staircase was the cocktail bar, through which one entered a large lounge bar. From this area, you could access the terrace and beer garden.

Whilst I had no understanding at this point in time of Competitive advantage, Market selection, Primary or Secondary opportunity, I later realised that Mr Walker was a skilled publican, hotelier and businessman. He had quantified the working men's bar as a continual source of income. His secret weapon: tremendous barmaids, as they were termed in the 60s, no political correctness here. Flirtatious, great fun, listener of confidences, however, do not touch. Pork crackling of an endless supply, beer nuts, and cheese. "They love the salt Philip, and it makes them drink more." I hope everyone is paying attention – specifically our health ministers.

First lesson – point of difference. The second lesson – walk like a King /Kipling etc. /Common touch. "Look after their wants and desires Philip and they will keep returning for more." He would spend his hour before lunch 11 am – 12 pm drinking with the men. He had a favourite Scotch, which was always kept on the 'top shelf' and we always knew that he liked to pour his own and he generally had a couple. It was Cold Tea. Yes, that is what I said, cold tea, absolutely brilliant. I later realised the term 'networking' had many derivatives to the normal expectation. I also saw many fail over the years because of alcohol-related employment. The third lesson – Never drink alcohol whilst at work (and I never did in 50 years) it may compromise you. Fourth lesson – Positive role model for your team. The cocktail at lunchtime was followed by a business lunch for the rich and famous, doctors, lawyers, heads of business etc. Dubonnet, pink gin, gin and tonic and quality scotch being the order of the day. Lunch and the table d'hôte menu were changed daily with fish always available, consistent quality food and service, always hosted by Mr and Mrs Walker. The fifth lesson – Mix with those that have the knowledge and subsequent power in the business community. You will grow your income stream and broaden your own knowledge bank.

The cocktail bar during the early evening served as a meeting place for businesspersons on the way home, those staying in the hotel and those having pre-dinner drink/cocktail drinks, prior to a show, lodge or dance. The large lounge was general patrons and Saturday/Friday nights became a meeting place for the young and aspiring, or 'those on their way to the Kirk' (Kirklevington Country Club). The car park was always full of Mercedes, Jaguar, RR, Bentley, Rover and Sprite, Morgan and MG to which I aspired to own one day.

Mr Walker (to everyone) was a tremendous mentor; giving constructive criticism, grateful acknowledgement of a job well done, and as I was to find out for the most part of my career, respected "attitude," someone that was prepared to go that extra yard. Hard work was an extremely well-regarded attribute. You also learned to work smarter, to achieve outcomes through others. Delegation – to gain respect from your team, often much older and more knowledgeable in their designated tasks.

I progressed through the mundane tasks required of a trainee (general dogs' body), early morning breakfast prep/commis assistant to the dining room, cellar support, tapping off, beer clarity and hygiene. Lunch, preparation, cooking support, sweeping the bar floors, empty ashtrays and wash. Wash crockery, cutlery, glassware and pots, lots of them. Bar support to the barmaids, more glasses, stack the cabinets, put away stock. I will not bore you further; let's say it was a multi-activity learning opportunity, greatly appreciated later. No demarcation here. It was a long day, broken with an afternoon off period. However, it still left time for fun during the course of the week. Paul (Marshal) and I now had our first girlfriends, Terrie and Gayle, both hairdressers – now that's a coincidence. Paul, Terrie and I were all the same age with Gayle maybe 19 or 20, some four years older. I seemed to prefer older women because all girlfriends later were all older and of course, Katie was born in 44. I'm not sure that's a good or a bad thing, maybe as a result of all my many surrogate mothers.

Our favourite music venue was the Redcar Jazz Club, or, if Paul and I could get in (we were not yet old enough to drink), The Kirk.

I remember my father giving me a 'subtle suggestion' one day which was often the case, given that outside of work I was a pain in the backside. The story follows:

Paul had just bought a 'Messerschmitt'. This was a three-wheeled, two-seater car with a motorcycle engine. As such, you could get your 'motor bike' licence, which permitted this form of 'car' at 16 years of age. Paul's mother and father (Elsie was one of my other motherly influences in my life, small, extremely funny and was an expert as to the qualities of Redcar fish and chip shops) They owned a driving school in Redcar, two minis (one Cooper) and an Anglia. Bill was also an excellent musician, playing the big thumper (double bass) in various bands or quartets, around the clubs and pub venues. They allowed a degree 'of slack' which we stretched to reach a tremendous old pub at Maske. A seaside town a short drive from Redcar. We would go for a drive in the Messerschmitt, attracting girl's attention, the objective being an illegal pint of stout at Maske and drive home. We always managed to get served, although we were both still extremely baby-faced. So, this sets the scene for fathers, "Watch your step, son."

Driving down through the Maske Bank with dad, showing me (as a passenger how to double de-clutch, gearing down). AKA, "you never rely on just your brakes Philip they may fail you. You must gear down, not missing a gear for the appropriate grade of the hill. Oh! Look son the Maske Pub. Have you ever been there?" No answer, I stayed shmuck. Pregnant pause. "I went into that pub when I was sixteen Philip, went to the bar to order a beer and then I saw them." Pause "Saw what Dad?" pause, "your grandfather's boots, I didn't hang around to get my pint." End of story.

This was my father's way of suggestive reasoning. You were on an imaginary lead, which was gradually lengthened, as he believed your independence increased. His objective being a self-sufficient, confident person, who was independent whilst at the same time, he was always available for support or advice if required. However, don't overstep, respect others rights and property. Basically, "Don't get too big for your shoes or you will be brought back to earth." I am deeply saddened to understand that many children today have no anecdotal tale let alone no father.

My employment knowledge improved, I worked hard and more than expected, listened carefully, observed a lot and asked many questions. I was given responsibility: in particular, control of monies, balancing sales to cash floats, until changeovers and preparation of monies for Mr Walker, ready for banking. The "old-timers" suggested that I was the first person, to their knowledge, to be allowed these tasks. I started to physically 'work' the bars, learning specific drink mixes, limited cocktails, control of cellar work, beer preparation, etc. I loved my work and I started to think that I may have a future. My problem was however profound, I hated Middlesbrough.

I have over my career paid particular attention to socio-economic/demographic profiles and whilst at 17, I did not understand why around 7% of the population were "peasants", as I thought of them, it registered. That was my term for those that got drunk, were foul-mouthed, often unemployed (the UK at that time was long into its second generation of welfare, supported by a significant group from the West Indies and Pakistan. Free medical, education, subsidised accommodation and welfare payments). I had grown up and schooled with Indians, Germans, Muslims and Jewish Poles who had all been displaced as a result of WWII. My father was extremely respectful of these persons, genuine refugees and indeed many of these types of migrants became neighbours. We had a German family three doors away and a Jewish newsagent. However, one characteristic separated these people from the non-wartime refugees. As such, they were well educated and had skills. They were as far as I was concerned just the same as us. Not so in many instances the non-war time economic opportunists to this day, I think that this period (mid 50's to mid60's) brought in many unskilled/economic refugees when unemployment was high, with local employment scarce in the North East. In my opinion, this added to the welfare burden dependency, a syndrome that prevails in Australia today and continues to grow. It magnifies the importance of education, employment and integration over periods of time and not on mass.

Whilst it will not happen in my life as politicians appear not to have the 'ticker' for a debate of tolerant realism. Required as to the positive and negative aspects of mass immigration into an area and the subsequent impact on all social structures, specifically the integration of mass culture, clearly vastly different to that which they have come from. Education, in my opinion, is a key issue whereby the migrant, not speaking the particular country's language, speak their own language at home, creating a natural difficultly for the children to adapt to and understand both school and culture. As such, in this situation the opportunity for marginalisation and the "drop out" of mainstream opportunities, creating more pressure on welfare structures and social cohesion. If the specific country has welfare. If not, then the associated issues occur in that particular society and international aid is required to house and feed these problems. It's said that politicians from democratic (or quazzy democracies) communist or dictatorship regimes have always created the environment for these circumstances to prevail, famine, war or natural environmental catastrophic and invariably it is someone "controlling for self-interest" the events which commonly make the situation worse. They say "good guys finish last", maybe this is why, for whatever is the reason, opposition whistle blowers or individual criticism get 'removed'. The Romans (Tiberius) did it, the British and French did it. Cromwell, Napoleon, Mussolini, Hitler, Amin, Mugabe, Moa, Suharto etc, to name but a few more recent well know characters. Whilst unfounded racism, white supremacists and nationality cleansing occur.

As a boy, I always dreamed, lost to my own thoughts and desires. If I could have a wish! Is there a God? Would I be granted a wish if I could see him? Do we have a parallel universe? If I could transcend time, could earthly molecular structure (my body) merge with cosmic molecular energy? Could I travel through time? Could I reach a speed of movement that enabled walking into another peaceful harmonious world encased in love, not control?

This led me to believe that I would need to test my theory. At 16, everything is possible. Regrettably, the right hand hurt like hell when I tried to pass it vertically through the kitchen table. As noticed in Charlie Chan movies, Kung Fu was clearly not the answer to astral travel, levitation or matter transfer.

Now in my 70's, I still dream of a humane earth. A 'we' mentality, independent, motivated, less constrained by capitalism ideology and the associated implications of consumptive desire, greed and power. Scarcity of resources. The influences of destruction. Whether that is deforestation, prohibition, war, overpopulation, pollution or starvation. That famous statement from whom we all remember is 'I have a dream'. Well, I have a dream. That all weapons would be destroyed. My one wish would be that at every attempt to produce any form of weapon, it would be transformed back to from where it came, the earth, a speck of dust particle physics at work.

Back to reality. I had an accident at work. I was slicing Gammon ham (bacon) for breakfast prep and instead of using (a) the guard and (b) the mesh glove; I sent the tip of my left thumb through the machine with the Gammon, thereby separating a section of thumb and nail from the rest of the hand. Very, very painful and unnecessary incident. I had been shown, told, and practised the procedure on numerous occasions. I was stupid. Self-preservation did not ignite the brain and my lack of personal discipline (and common sense) resulted in unnecessary pain. It was my fault, nobody else's. No bloated health and safety Public Service regimes, no melodrama and no social media photographs. No posting to my 1450 "friends" as to what I had done. It was an 'I' moment, not a 'me' tirade, "I was a bloody irresponsible little brat." So, it was off to the doctors with Mr Walker. "Are you Okay Philip, are you feeling faint?" The hand swathed in every bandage from the first aid box. Of course, I was feeling faint, what a daft question, could he not see that I was at death's door?

My hand looked like a Primo Carneros hand, then a heavyweight boxer, bandaged, prior to the glove fitting and the heavyweight bout at the Middlesbrough Gym. Hospital, stitches, a bandage and its home to ponder my; 'feeling sorry for myself'. This was my second major disruption to boys will be boys. The first was caused by Jimmy, some years before, with his new bow and arrow set, with a rubber tip to the arrows, so you could not hurt anyone or thing.

No gaming for us, no Pokémon, it was old-fashioned cowboys and Indians. Circa: seven years old. I was the cowboy (remember I had the horse) and Jimmy was Chief Sitting Bull. I had the gun with noise caps and it was my intention to kill this brat half breed. Well, not really, that was just off dreaming and imagination. Not, however, good for the intended prosperity for our indigenous inhabitants, kill or be killed, and still no Indigenous Charter!

Back to the accident, you see, we realised that if we removed the rubber cap from the head of the arrow, we could sharpen the tip with our penknife. All boys had to have a penknife. One never knew when a buffalo, lion or wilder beast might come out of the trees into the back garden of suburban "Brookfield Gardens" in the cold heart of the north of England. However, Jimmy mistook me for a lion and shot me above the right eye. Crying-boys used to do that in those days, I ran into the bedroom to inform my mother that I never wished to see Jimmy again. That it wasn't fair, I was supposed to kill him. I was the cowboy, the white one. My mother fainted which made my situation worse. So, it's off to Jimmy's mother, a bandage and lap around the head bandage. Jimmy got a clip around the ear from his dad, the bow and arrow were destroyed and I became the hero.

Then dad came home. I was no longer the wounded warrior, I was a 'stupid bugger' who, by now should start to 'grow up' and act like a McLean.

So back to the hotel after the hand incident, back at work within two days. "Yes, Mr Walker thank you, yes, I am fine, no I really want to come back, I can work with one hand, anything."

"Okay Philip, however, please be extremely careful till your thumb is healed. Suck it up kid, no health and safety bureaucracy, litigations mentality or Public Service here. No standing in queues, filling out forms, solicitors and autocracy. Ultimately today a number, a utility and a pawn in their little game of control – your personal independence removed. Your caring bureaucracy." I continued to work hard, listening, practice and learn.

Paul passed his driving licence, sold the Messerschmitt and bought a car. A Morris Oxford. He was now in his 1st year of apprenticeship as a motor mechanic with Pendleton's Garage on the Esplanade at Redcar. Eric Pendleton was Terrie's father. Incidentally, I spent time with him on his 94th in Whitby, 2018, still as sharp as a tack. Sadly, he separated from Terrie's mother, Joan, a feisty vivacious woman of maybe 34/35. Who at 15 years old, I was madly in lust with? In my dreams. Joan owned a salon, Maison Terrie, on Station Street. Quite a large salon, staff, Terrie and Gayle. Paul and I, as trainee painters and decorators (looking for more pocket money), offered to paint the salon on nights or days when the salon was closed. We completed the process and were pleased with our skill, workmanship and cleanliness. We had no option, we had been placed in families where you had to tidy up or no pocket money, it's that simple. You only receive when you give.

My memory is somewhat hazy at this point, so Paul if you read this and I get it wrong, I apologise.

We were taking the car out for a test run. Paul, as usual, had been doing mechanical things, for which he was extremely competent and methodical. We were driving towards Great Ayton/Guisborough where Paul's elder sister, Sheila lived. The next section is what I was told, as I have no recollection then or to this day as to what happened. The car came over the crest of a hill and was confronted with a car travelling towards us and turning right into a lane directly across our path. Paul hit the brakes to no avail; the Oxford hit the other car. Windscreens in those days did not 'shatter' as they do today and there were no seatbelts. Consequently, I was catapulted into and through the sharded windscreen. The engine was pulled to the left, so that, whilst I believe in and have always worn seatbelts since implementation, if I had been wearing one, I would possibly have been killed. Paul was badly bruised and shaken; the driver of the other car was killed.

I was taken to Teesside General Hospital unconscious and fortunately, for me, a specialist plastic surgeon was visiting the hospital. A long operation followed 400 stitches to the head, a rebuilt nose (leg cartilage) and the left eye popped back into the socket. The result was 'the invisible man', with one eye and mouth visible. I regained consciousness the next day to find my father sleeping by the bed; my watch had stopped at 1:03 pm on Sunday, and this was Monday.

To digress slightly this was the first divining moment of my life and now, looking back, I realise that I have been blessed or lucky or both. I have had highs I have had lows, yet, whatever seems to have been thrown at me, I have always come out okay and grateful. Someone was looking out for me or something.

My body was black and blue, I was extremely sore although I recollect no great pain. I had a constant stream of visitors all feeling sorry for poor Philip. I then started to feel sorry for 'poor Philip'. Always hyperactive, staying in bed did not please a young boy keen to get back to work. This was not productive, nor income-producing, not ensuring that the bar was kept clean, well-stocked and tidy.

No, I could not get up yet, no, I could not have a shower. You will be washed in bed and, wait for it, it's the bedpan. Do you think I am going to let a spunky young nurse (all of 19) see me do my business lying in a bed, never? "Be quiet Philip, just get on with it, otherwise it will be the suppository?" God, help me.

Now it just happened that the fellow in the opposite bed had wheels. The answer to confinement, borrow the wheelchair, enabling a full review of all nurses on the ward night and day. Margaret was especially nice. Hayden Oakley's older sister (21). I was soon put into my 16-year-old place. However, she did accompany me to the toilet in the wheelchair and my first test of broken arrogance. Stretching up from the chair to look at my wounds in the washroom mirror. My halo became instantly dislodged. Little Lord Fauntleroy had disappeared and terror took hold. What I saw was Frankenstein, a bandaged dried blood-soaked monster, not the good-looking delicate boned pretty Charles's son. A moron Dickensian character from the gutters of poverty. I was devastated.

Margaret got it, I didn't. So, the suggestion was a walk to another ward to get some fresh air. "Please don't worry Philip, you have been extremely lucky, it will all heal, you had a wonderful surgeon." You are extremely lucky; there goes that word again, luck. What is luck when you fly through a windscreen and wreck your 'pretty face' for life? That's not luck, that is the end of the world. There were five bodies, all deadly still and black, drips, tubes, pipes and all manner of paraphernalia and moaning. The stench of burning flesh clung to the air as fans aimed to cool these charred bodies, which 24 hours prior, had been happy normal people, wives, girlfriends, children and friends, unaware of what was to occur.

It was an explosion and fire. Made worse, it was a chemical fire at ICI Chemical Plant, the stinking behemoth that pumped out acrid smoke choking the lungs of the unsuspecting populate of Middlesbrough, Stockton and further dependant on which way the winds blew. Global warming was not an issue; Sir David Attenborough was only a young man and the world's powerful men required petrochemical bi-products at any cost. Smoking, that was good for you, it relieved stress and through ingenious marketing suggestion, made you feel suave. How stupid we are as a species of supposed intellect to blindly follow. Or, is it called addiction? Maybe intended consequences.

Margaret whispered that three men may not live given the extent and damage caused by the burns to lungs and legs, not a sight that I would recommend unless of course you are a little spoilt brat only thinking of your own ego and self-pity. If you have all of those character traits, I hastily recommend it.

To this day, it had an unimaginative impression as though a light was switched on as I realised that there were many people with worse disabilities than mine in my illness or indeed general life. So, stop acting like a goose and get away from these negative thoughts.

Over the weeks, the bandages were removed, the nose plugs "pulled out" and the eyes tested. I now had light coverings of bandage and plaster, able to shower, walk and finally the stitches were removed. Slowly, the men from ICI died, only one remained and slowly improved. I wore my scars with pride and after seven weeks 'still bandaged lightly', I convinced Mr Walker to allow me to come back to work. Cellar, kitchen, anything. He was wonderful, still remembering the war, its destruction and subsequent injuries. You could not feel sorry for people, concerned yes, understanding, yes, however, never sorry. No dumb tweets, just honesty.

The scars healed, a large section under my hair could not be seen, and however, one scar on my left side and across the bridge of the nose opened up conversation opportunities. The eye would 'wander' to the centre and it was quite hilarious whilst talking to someone and, because of the apparent line of sight of that eye, the persons spoken to would, looking concerned, keep wiping their nose. Clearing, thinking that something was 'hanging there'. It also showed how self-conscience a person can become, and indeed, how destructive it can be to self-esteem unless remedied. Slowly and with a number of years, I became extremely comfortable in my own body and I hope without arrogance, always have been. What you see is what you get, if you don't like it, tough. Maybe at 24/25 years of age. I am however deeply saddened today, specifically with social media, girls and young women who become "body-conscious" for all the wrong reasons. Negativity being their stimuli, not as I encountered. Plastic surgery – the moon face, pouting, Botox or breast augmentation. Very, very, sad, saying little to the type of male species that accept this manipulation. Beauty is inside and lust is limited.

My employment continued its upward course, and whilst I did not appreciate it at the time, the depth of training I reccived. It was indeed the building blocks that enabled me to enjoy the tremendous career that I eventually progressed to.

I despair today and indeed the latter part of my career, whereby business activities or corporations reduce their training and development budgets to balance the books with one major objective, shareholder dividend/wealth. It has been well documented over the years (and ignored) that CEO's who concentrate on the consumer, trading statement activity and employee's motivation, produce far greater shareholder wealth and consistent growth trending than those focused totally on the share price.

I was restless; I had broken off with Gayle and a number of 'girlfriends' pleased little. I hated Middlesbrough and that was not going to change. I wanted something more, however, I did not know what I wanted. I didn't want 'a job for life' in polluted little old Middlesbrough. I wanted to be different, to achieve greater meaning in life, to be someone special. However, I did not know who I wanted to be, more importantly, I didn't know how to achieve that objective. Aunt Nan's life projection, desires and dreams created visions, however, not the means or capacity as how to get there. Work ethic was a quality recommendation;

however, that alone was not going to get me what I was trying to find. I was a very confused young man.

At the hotel, I was a well-dressed employee, hardworking, extremely quick at satisfying customer needs, incredibly polite and sometimes reserved, all that I had been taught by my extended loving family of surrogate mothers, aunts, uncles and grandmother. However, outside of work, I was becoming sometimes uncouth, smoking, drinking and 'big-headed'. It was no reflection on my friends, it was me. I started wearing 'cheaper' different clothes, not the style or class that had been the norm when guided in my mid-teens by grandmother or Aunt Nan. Quality was replaced with quantity and my dressing reflected the images of the now famous 'teddy boy', without the motorbike.

I went up to Scotland for a few days as Aunt and Uncle had moved to Dalkeith, an outskirt commuter suburb of Edinburgh. Both working, still not owning a house and aunt still spending uncle's paycheque as soon as it was received. I had a quick re-education of self-improvement; quality and I have no doubt they were concerned as to the direction I was apparently heading.

Chris had gone down to Cambridge after completing his O's and A's and, with grandmother, he was held as the role model to which I could aspire. I now paid little attention; however, Uncle discussed Napier College, a new polycentric in Edinburgh. Greg was planning to study at the Scottish Hotel School – Strathclyde University. Napier was a facility with hotel school operations, Reception, Housekeeping, Dining room, Bedroom and both commercial and short order kitchens. It was a hands-on practical application with theory appropriate to City and Guilds diplomas in hospitality and a Higher National Certificate for Hotel Management. Obviously, I listened and was soon enrolled at Napier, with the intent of living with aunt and uncle who had now moved to Penicuik, another commuter suburb.

My resigning from the Linthorpe hotel was both a shock to Mrs and Mrs Walker and myself. They were extremely gratuitous and grateful for my work ethic and wished me well with my new endeavour. I kept in touch for many years and it was only after some time that indeed as I had been told, not having children of their own, they had actually seen me as someone who could ultimately take over responsibility for their business. Yet another lesson in life, give people the appropriate training and responsibility as their skills develop, trust them with decision making, leaving the door open for constructive critique. Most importantly tell them when they have performed well. I would add, as I was told:

never confront a team member, never lose your patience and never ever berate someone in front of anybody else. Ever.

2) Observations of a Scatter Brain: College, Canada, Louise Zoo's and Kangaroos

Enter Sam Denzler, Chef extraordinaire, Swiss mother and German father, Senior Lecturer: practical and theory. Paris trained, Escoffier and his only bible, Le Repertoire De La Cuisine, first published in Paris 1914 by Monsieur L Saulnier. It was the standard by which the very best would be judged and Sam was like a regimental sergeant major on steroids. He took no prisoners, if you left a Sabatier (knife) in the sink or added greens to the ever-ready stockpot, lookout. The reverse of Chef Denzler was Chef Henry Winston who, traditionally trained, was far more relaxed. Incidentally, he was Katie's lecturer in 'large scale preparation', while she was studying Industrial catering at Athol Crescent, of course, that was all in the future.

I enjoyed college, the work ethic in pracs and the theory in lectures. I shone through and because of my foundry work/farmyard career/car protection racket, hairdressing aspirant and of course, the Linthorpe Hotel, I possibly had a little lead on many. So, once more I became a know it all, it seemed to possess me, a know it all, yet knowing nothing of real substance.

I made friends very easily and there was soon a group of newfound companions that shared similar values and aspirations. I had moved to Penicuik, however, soon decided to move into a flat with some of my friends. Where I got the money from, I have no recollection, grandmother no doubt, my father and my casual work in various pubs, but I'm not sure. However, somehow, I managed to pay the rent at 10 quid a week. Food prepared and tested in college became the food bowl; baked beans, boiled egg and bread with marmalade became the norm in the flat.

Colin Scott-Smith got a job as a 'delivery driver' between lectures and would arrive back to the flat with 'damaged stock' of such items there were great quantities of canned herring in tomato sauce. Absolutely broke and no food, we lived off this canned mileage and college tastings for weeks. I have never eaten canned herrings since. Martin Murray, whose parents lived in Paisley and father was the local doctor, always seemed to get money from home, so we were always borrowing a couple of quid until we got some money. His aunt was Greer Garson the American actress, consequently, we were all quite envious as to his aunt's presents. He did however share. Scott-Smith's parents were domiciled accountants in Beirut and they kept a beautiful, more importantly, a well-stocked house at Crief, so this was occasionally a source of provisions. Specifically, his old man's well-stocked Scotch selection and Cuban Havana's.

We were coming up to our first vacations and it was expected that any student would find appropriate work within the hospitality industry in Edinburgh. Written submissions as part of the course expectation would record specific aspects of work experience and the particular topic chosen, disseminating workplace activities.

Greg secured a future holiday position at the George Hotel and it was expected that I would follow suit, maybe the North British or Caledonian Hotels. I had other ideas, London sounded good, maybe the Carlton, Ritz, Hilton or Dorchester? I raised the subject with Chef and he said he would sanction London if I could find a position. I was delighted, I was on my way again. The Adlib Club, the Establishment, girls and beer, here I come. That idea soon changed. Whilst working as a commis, outside of lectures for work experience, I spoke to one of the Queen's travelling chefs and he told me that great opportunities and money were possible (once exams were completed). To join the Royal household with secure employment, accommodation, travel and higher than industry wages. Now, it just happened that a friend, Angus was the Queen's fifth cousin or something like that. He sounded like the Queen when he spoke, drove a Sunbeam Spitfire and was never short of money. Yes, what I had been told was correct, however, to attain a position on the Royal Yacht (Britannia) was the jewel in the crown. World travel, higher than available plus salary, I was in. I already had the job, the mind regenerated, ideas formed. Why not apply for a position with a cruise ship operation during vacation? But where airlines becoming the new favoured mode of travel. More expensive, passenger shipping was in decline unless you were migrating to Canada, Australia or South Africa. Canada, now that's a thought.

Uncle George and Aunt Pat, Chris and Jennifer's mother and father had moved to Canada. Uncle had been in the merchant navy and whilst I had seen little of him, given the distance to which they had moved. On those occasions, I always remember a man with a story of adventure. I recollect, as a young teenager being advised, "I should never be as silly to get a tattoo," and that "I must work and study hard to get my papers."

Subsequently, I contacted the Canadian Pacific Steamships office in Liverpool and received a favourable response. I discussed it with a few of my student mates and eventually (I think) it was five or six that approached the college and the opportunity was subsequently approved – if we could secure acceptance. That was duly given and we were advised that we must however join the Merchant Seaman's Union.

The ship designated was the Empress of Canada, plying weekly passage from Liverpool through Newfoundland into the St Laurence River, Quebec (Hotel Frontenac) and Montreal (Hotel Champlain).

As is often the case in my youth, I lost interest in college. I am reading Captain Morgan, The Pirates of the Caribbean, Jamaica, Trinidad, etc. and I am once more consumed with dreaming, all I can think about is going to sea.

Finally, the end of term arrives and we are off kitbag, whites, blacks, formals and casuals. I cannot remember how I got to Liverpool, hitchhiked on train or bus, nonetheless arrived in one piece. Induction was at the wharf offices and introduction to our "boss", the ship's purser, known as Rock Hudson. Possibly because he was a big handsome man or that he was clearly and openly gay; quite a rarity in Middlesbrough, more obvious in Edinburgh.

We were advised of our responsibility, that we would be treated like any member of the regular ship's crew, stay out of trouble, don't miss the ship when she leaves port, work hard and don't catch the 'clap'. For such a smart arse know it all, I was laughed at from the room when I asked what the clap was, the tag stayed with me for some time and became the object of Phil jokes. Later – let me just say – that she was not wearing knickers.

We were shown our quarters, six bunks to a room, communal showers and toilet, the brig (pub) and crew cafeteria.

Al (Alistair) and I were designated first-class with initial duties (commis waiter) reporting to that specific table waiter. I remember little of the general daily routine except to say if you were allocated a 'good table', you received better tips. The Captain's table being the optimum. Basic pay was 14 quid a week, 12 hours a day, 7 days a week. In the first passage, I made approximately 70 quid in tips, however, as the 'rooky', I was expected to provide anything that was not listed on the menu duly requested by the guest. My first allocated table was a wealthy Canadian (Irish migrants) family, three children, a nanny and a teacher. By way of example, if fruit for breakfast was: orange, banana, melon and they wanted grapes; it was my responsibility to ensure provision.

It was my first experience of corruption and theft (by officers of a company from that company) and later in my career became a focus in retail for security and the theory being 'keep the honest from temptation, catch and remove the guilty'.

The process was to request from the particular chef departie, the menu ingredient item required dependant on the nature, cost and availability. Caviar could be ten shillings, filet mignon, seven and sixpence, grapes sixpence, Stilton a shilling and so forth. Consequently, my 70 pounds in tips reduced to 30. The monies, in this instance, was put into the 'tronk', and shared amongst the departie, dependant on status within the galley and dining room.

So much for British integrity, ethics, honesty and loyalty. It was all very new to me and I started to appreciate that I was not actually as bad as I thought, or indeed as most of my family thought of me.

It was wonderful exposure by the day's standards; we earned quite good money and gained valuable experience. Not least independence and maturity. The ship, the Frontenac and the Champlain all gave hospitality insight into a different world. Certainly, far better culinary offering than traditionally found in UK Hotels.

Theme and image influenced decisions in design, many years later for me a pursuit and something, I still hold dear today. Bring the consumer or guest into the food experience. The Champlain had a number of restaurants, one of which opened into butchery, hanging and ageing room, bakery (the smells), short-order cook and prep (as with theatre), to the immediate attention of the diner. Choose your cut; select your fish (swimming) and your cheese. Let the Sommelier then suggest your wine according to degustation or bespoke menu choice. Then watch your dining preparation. It's a common occurrence now, extremely rare then. More exposure.

It was on one such passage that I was given my sexual ritual. Up to that point any girlfriends that I may have had allowed little in the way of sexual desires of a normal teenage boy. The best that a wondering hand could manage was a light breast touch, if you were lucky. Legs of the day consisted of stockings, suspenders, petticoats and the 'vice' pose. That was, forget it Charlie, its marriage first or nothing. A vice-like action would occur and if one had a hand misplaced in the perceived indirect position, the 'vice movement' could have taken the handoff if one had not been quick enough.

I was extremely quick and well-practised because of the 'vice' movement on many occasions. Sadly, for my dreams, that is all that happened. A number of sailors decided that we (the students), needed a little 'street smarts' sexual training.

This involved an invitation to a bar on the waterfront in Quebec, which held Jazz performances. The Jazz opportunity sounded excellent, therefore, after shift off we went, oblivious as to what this specific venue was. I had visions of a French-speaking Redcar jazz club. I still had a lot of growing up to do. We sat down and a very attractive and scantily clad young lady duly approached for drink orders. I ordered a beer and paid her. However, she stood there and stood there, I was trying to determine the reason when a seaman advised that she was waiting for her tip (the cost of the beer in my case). She smiled while I gave her the money, stroked my hair and said I was beautiful. I smiled, thanked her, and she walked back to the bar, to riotous laughter from the seafaring customers.

And the comments – hey she wants you, Phil. Clean white flesh. Look at her, she is desperate. I looked towards the bar and there she sat legs apart and no knickers on. No vice movement here. It was on full show. There was however one problem, all the girls were doing the same thing. It was a brothel. Al and I finished our beer and left, much to the jeers of our seafaring mates.

When we arrived back at our dock in Liverpool, I had to ask when going to the pay office to collect our pay, why there were two lines, one leading to a separate room. It was one for your pay and one for the 'Jab'. To this end, I still remained a virgin with no clap. A much-preferred option.

This stay in the dock was called a 'turnaround' and as my designated college assignment: 'provisioning a passenger ship' I stayed on board to watch and record the procedures. All seamen left for shore leave and day wharf crews arrived. There was maintenance to be done and provisions to be loaded.

The purser, Rock Hudson, stayed on board for the four days, overseeing the various activities. In my case looking at stock arriving, counting and recording goods. The huge quantities to feed 1200 passengers and the crew for weeks was something to behold. The provisions just kept coming, classified and transferred to the appropriate cool room, freezer, kitchen, bar, housekeeping stores etc. Something strange occurred. The goods and provisions moved up a conveyer belt from the dock into a companion door, quite high up from the Plimsoll line on the side of the ship. Goods moved continually and it took a considerable number of the shore crew and the wharfies to complete the tasks. However, as a good transferred in, a good came out of a small companion door closer to the waterline. There was always a small van or car loaded with stock and off it drove. Various public service personnel seemed to be involved. Off duty seamen and customs police. Uncle Tom Cobbly and all appeared to be a party to the activity.

This was my first real experience of theft and corruption on a large and well-organised scale, orchestrated by individuals under the noses of the officers of Canadian Pacific. Indeed, any experience of theft and corruption, this had not been in this boy's training to date. It angered me. Why? Was it something in my upbringing, something in the upbringing that identified as wrong? Rough, uncouth petty criminals, it was all so obvious and unchecked, again, the peasants in life. Want to take stolen duty-free alcohol or cigarettes ashore through the crew, simple money or goods and that was it. Just steal from your employer.

The illegal drug culture was just gaining momentum in university cities within the UK and whilst I never saw this at Canadian Pacific, I often wonder how many drugs came in through this process. My father told me these types of persons, working-class heroes were: 'the salt of the earth'. To me they were definitely peasants, stealing from the hand that fed them, whilst simultaneously reducing the profit margin available to their company and future. That thought, the profit margin concept would transpire later.

I determined that I was going to learn inventory and stock control. I was going to design systems that reduced the opportunity to steal. That came quite some years later, nonetheless, it came. I called it productivity and product profiling (PPP) driven by percentages rather than dollars or units. It entered the calculation of what food was purchased at cost. What that product cost to produce, sell and what the difference was. The difference being, that wasted, damaged, over portioned or stolen. Very simple in theory, however, not in the text at that point in time. Computing now produces profiles to behold.

Our term as seamen came to an end; we had experienced many new things in life, not to forget our last trip out of St Lawrence. The last ship to leave before ice-clogged this vast waterway for the winter, following the Alexander Pushkin. An icebreaker preceded the Pushkin as we weaved our way around ice flows and rouge icebergs some (underwater) as large a mass as the ship. For those who have not experienced this, an iceberg is 1/3 above water 2/3 below. The Empress was an "Atlantic Class" which meant that she would sail in extremely rough weather conditions. Today's cruise liners, top-heavy and with no California bow would never be allowed to venture into this maelstrom. This, our last passage, was 'batten down' and all passengers to their cabins. Was it rough, one minute 300 feet on top of a wave the next underwater? I loved it. We continually looked after passengers most of whom were seasick. I can't say that at times, I was not scared, however, "old sea dogs" kept reassuring me that they had been through worse.

The ship took one hell of a battering and once back at Liverpool dock, I could see the damage to forwarding derricks, bow, rails and so forth. When you realise that the ocean is in control, whilst waves can buckle six-inch steel plate you soon learn a healthy, self-preservation attitude and respect for her.

We said our farewells and headed back to Napier and normality. It gave me a lifelong respect for seamen and women, regrettably not so wharfies.

This was the start of love and respect for both sailing and the ocean. Not however large ships, rushed short schedules, today's sheep pen accommodation and herd mentality, not to mention continuous food tourism. Our ships were small to moderate-sized cruisers, V8 powered, double bed, galley, bathroom and always a large back deck. Fishing took hold, moments to relax, contemplate and consider for over 40 years.

Back at Napier, I forget where I was staying at the time, I bought a car. A little sports car called 'I think' a Bolwell or something similar. It was what was called a kit car and was classified as a 'Poormans Sportscar' if you could not afford the real thing. I had learnt to drive initially on the farm at Egton Bridge, tractor and Land Rover on the farm tracks and paddock. Today I believe a great way for young people to get the feel for a motor vehicle. Three-point turns, hill starts, doubled clutch, hand brake skids – all perfected in relative speed and safety. One gains confidence in man or woman and the vehicle. You get to know how far you can stretch the envelope, your delicate invincibility and oft-stupid action, all safely away from others.

So, it's off to the streets of Edinburgh, wind in the hair, sheepskin, scarf and beanie. Aunt and Uncle were impressed, they loved the car and said, "Was the insurance expensive, Philip?"

"Oops, no! I haven't got that yet, Uncle."

"What! You do have your driving licence?"

'Err not yet uncle, next week'. Once more, I shatter expectations. I always seem to break rules, and unfortunately, outside of work, it's always bucking the system. As they say in Australia 'up your bum', why be the same as everyone else? I'm different. I was actually the peasant, not caring for anyone, except myself. Stuff everyone, no matter how many you let down – just look after no one.

In the mid-'70s, I drove up to Longniddry to where Aunt and Uncle were living at the time. In a hire car (with Katie and Lou) on holiday from Australia and the first thing, my uncle said was "Hello Philip," looking at the car and smiling, "do you have a driving licence yet?"

Life continued. I sometimes think that a reason for college time was that I was fed. I'm sure that if I had chosen art, I would have become a life model in skeletal form. However, as always, l managed to "secure monies" for cigarettes. They had to be black Russian Sibrani and my drink of preference had gravitated from Guinness to gin and tonic. Not the ideal combination for a starving, penniless student becoming more like his aunt than his grandmother. Aunt spent everyone else's money; grandmother never spent anything on herself. Opposites: daughter, spendthrift, Mother, extremely thrifty, whilst unbelievably generous with family, especially me, I could convince her of anything which would result in more 'borrowings'.

"Now Philip, you promise you won't tell your father?"

"No Gran,"

"And no one else."

"Definitely not. Thank you, I will pay you back."

I have few regrets in my life, one however always haunts me. I never did have the time to pay her back financially, more importantly for the attention I was given, constructive criticism and all tough love. In the mid-seventies when I last saw her (well into her 80's) she was showing signs of dementia and the conversation was often followed as to, if I was Chris, Greg or Phil. She had grown up with the Wright brothers, Clippers to Dreadnoughts. Horse and cart to cars and I'm not sure she really appreciated what a Boeing 747 was or its impact on travel aspirations. She died shortly afterwards and this was one fine lady to whom I never paid my dues. As stated,

Quote 'Woman hold up half the sky – Mao Zedong.'

This woman certainly held up my world for quite some time.

As she always said, "Never a borrower nor lender be." She certainly broke her own rule with me. One aspect of the vacant journey, one often never lives to experience, final years of loved ones in the birth country.

While my father was diagnosed with terminal lung cancer, Katie and I enjoyed a wonderful holiday with Win and Charles plus the Clarkin clan and outlaws in Mallaig, Scotland. This was in 1991. By 1992, I had three flights booked, back and forth to be with him. I only made the two trips the second being to say my goodbyes and funeral. Fortunate that (a) we could afford the expense and (b) that I worked in a wonderful work environment with colleagues who covered my meetings and objectives superbly. Again, the migratory dilemma, life's love lost.

The college had become boring again and I now fell in love. Real love, maybe lust, put quite simply – sex. My virginity had been broken by a highly sexual 2nd-year medical student for reasons of potential embarrassment I will not name – my sex goddess. She probably became a respected retired Harley St specialist, great mother, grandmother indeed now, possibly great-great-grandmother. It occurred in a one-room student bedsit near Greyfriars Bobby, our local pub. No vice action here, after meeting her at a hash arranged party in the grass market. Over the coming weeks, we spent many hours in bed. Her on "special smokes" (I have never touched illicit drugs) and me, my Black Russian. Music namely Cohen, Cale, Dylan, Crawdaddy, Thomas, Who, Pentangle, and Bonzo Dog. Fuelled with cheap Chianti and Wimpy burgers. Her anatomy specimens in formaldehyde encroached the space. Concerning when one such specimen was a rather erect penis generally sitting next to my pillow in full view of our experimentation, in a jar.

No longer a boy but a worldly man, travelled and monies (grandmothers), I soon realised that my newfound love was not to be my future; she was accommodating a number of scheduled dalliances with others, including Martin's elder brother. What a prick, I should have kept my big mouth shut. I looked for greener pastures and many followed. Hell, it was the 60s, free love, rebellion, Vietnam, we were about to land a man on the moon.

At a humungous cost of capitalist excess, Kennedy and Khrushchev had discussed joint commitment and the future potential end of the cold war. Nonetheless, the wall came later, much later, such as the speed of political will.

Kennedy was assassinated and Khrushchev was ousted. So that was that. American democratisation and image held steady and to the gaze of the world's herd in true capitalist failure. A few made billions and the herd got a story of imagination. We will be on Mars in ten years and next – outer space. We are still trying and will continue to do so, creating economic opportunity for the few: whilst maintaining that dream of going to space in "a tin can strapped to a very large bomb." Molecular structure, bridging time and physics, is our only hope. The Hedron is a start, and, specifically as China plans the largest ever by 2028. Beam me up Scotty, that's where our future lies.

Once more, my life took a new turn, this time in the form of a respectable religious gathering near Brunswick. I knew a few of those present, mainly students, town planning, philosophy, medical and after the usual formalities and drinks, I sauntered over to a rather shy, slim looking female. A white dress, more like a bridesmaid than the usual student garb.

I asked her which college she attended and she told me she had studied at Athol Crescent. Had then worked for various companies and finally at McVities Bakery and Café on Princess as manageress. However, had left hospitality and now managed the 'Sewing Centre' opposite Norway House.

We talked, transcendental, Maslow – it was easy, relaxed and we clearly had similar tastes, and before I realised, it was quite late. I reached for another glass of cheap red (my drink of choice now as gin and tonic proved both too expensive for grandmothers' budget and left me with a pounding headache). The glass left the hand and in a slow knowing direction covered the front of her beautiful white creation. Sorry, I forgot to mention Catherine Mary Clarkin (known to friends, never the family, as Katie.) Well, that did it, she was whisked away by friends, saturated and I left in mild disgrace.

I don't recollect how or where, as history shows, we met somewhere else. The long meaningful conversations ensued, I took her out to various venues and pubs, including the 'Golf links Hotel' across the green from where she flatted with others – Warrender Park Terrace. Clearly, there was some chemistry between us and she advised that she was a single mother, that the baby's father had deserted her prior to birth.

Expecting an abortion, her family, staunch Catholics had all but disowned her; it was the era of the contraception pill or an abortion, if you got caught unprotected. Similarly, as in many cases, the child was adopted out. From a strict

Catholic Scottish/Irish background, no support with birth was given, as the pill, abortion or adoption was not an alternative for her or her upbringing. The hospital gave her the adoption papers and she refused to sign them. The baby, Louise, was now approximately 14 months old. I was not particularly interested; I was only interested in Katie. Until I was finally invited back to the flat to meet the others, and Louise. Then, and only God know why, this bundle of giggles grew on me.

My intimacy with Katie increased and we sat for hours during the evening discussing all manner of topics. We had the same likes and dislikes, the same food taste (except Mollusc or shellfish in general, an annoying experience to date). We appreciated the same music; our only variance was our taste in clothes. Mine was now the House of Fraser – hers was homemade and 'flowery'. A budgetary requirement for a totally unsupported single mother.

I moved in to live with her. Katie's flatmate consisted of the tenancy leaseholder, Ian, a habitual student, who was never intended to complete study. A chess addict, who rarely went to bed prior to 4:00 am and rarely rose till 4:00 pm, lived on biscuits and cheese and as I recollect, favoured readings such as Mien Camp or the Karma Sutra. Flagellation all tried and tested on Margaret, his part-time girlfriend and nurse. His father was the Ambassador to Norway and he seemed to think that one day, with two or three degrees, the public system and his father's contacts would ensure his pension. Well-read in broader terms he was nonetheless one of those persons that could ensure lengthy meaningful student conversations. He was great company. Others invariably bedded the extra two rooms, supplementing the general rent requirement.

Katie paid 10 pounds per week plus utilities and once again, I paid nothing. Her wage was 14 pounds per week, which left little for nursery and food. Consequently, any monies I earned or borrowed became a lifeline for the higher expectations of life, good food and wine. Albeit, that generally we ended with Chianti, a cheap acceptable option whilst one dreamt of what could be. Specifically, when daily routines at college brought into focus 'the top shelf' opportunities.

I adored Louise and spent hours with this little thing. She gave me a purpose and whilst what she said at that point made little sense. I was 'Pill', Pill this Pill that. I would pick her up from nursery or take time out to go on an excursion, exploring areas with the pram at breakneck speed around the lanes and alleyways of Edinburgh. I started to play a significant role in her behaviours, manners and the like. I'm not sure I knew at the time, given that parenting is both a huge responsibility and indeed an often-steep learning curve. I had never given a damn about anyone except me at an early age and it deeply saddens, concerns and annoys to see youth today, well into their late twenty, totally focused on their narcissistic self-ways past their youth and growing up years. I remember a common comment in the McLean household, which was 'what's a marrar' to which I would be told, English is important son if you use it correctly. It is "what's the matter?" So today, when I hear, "My brother and me," or "he done it," "the women ran across road, or a woman walked alone." Not understanding the e or a consequently I set about teaching this baby the English language with my limited capacity.

Supporting a child in their upbringing is not an easy procedure, especially when that child is not biologically yours and you are not linked to the mother in an objective long-term relationship, and more appropriately, you are a penniless student. In that period, that meant marriage. How could I possibly adapt to that scenario and not continue to let people down? Katie, as a single mother tended to give easily to a baby's demands. Let's face reality here, a baby soon learns to stretch the boundaries, the chocolate box is only a short reach away. "Suck it up you, dumbass adult, give me what I want, otherwise I will bawl the house down and I will have you charged with neglect of my wants. And, I'm only 14 months old, just wait until I get to 14 years." Consequently, never to this day believe in the psychological babble of 'unconditional love', I established some boundaries, "If you are hurt I will find a doctor who will heal you, if you are lonely I will comfort you, if you are scared I will console you and, if anyone tries to hurt you I will protect you." However, don't think that by bawling your eyes out in a tantrum, you will get what you want. Guess what, you won't win. This set the scene for a battle of will over a chocolate biscuit.

A baby in my life started to make me realise that as we developed and grew into adulthood, you had to become responsible for your actions, which in a parent's objective must be to your ability to create survival instinct, independence not dependency. To do this you are required guidance, council, constructive critique, boundaries, no go zones, support, parental not hypocritical parents and tons of love and affection. That the consistent personal and smart work habits and that your role model, both female and male, form the structure as to how your child developed. In a take no prisoner, dog eat dog capitalist environment.

You had to learn to be adaptive and try to solve your own problems and most critically to feel comfortable in your own body and persona. You have to accept your mistakes in trying not to make the same again. You have to gain stamina and self-confidence, not narcissist arrogance. You have to develop empathy, natural generosity and caring concern. Not so as public service authorities, who orchestrate care programs for specific needs, whilst in actual reality embody simple 'service departments'.

Our lives continued as a financial struggle, not unusual in a student city, until once again divine intervention or luck, came in the form of an unexpected trust account, created as a compensation payment for the car accident's 'pain and suffering'. I had not been aware of these intentions. By today's standards, it was not a large amount of monies, nonetheless worth consideration. I clearly had a lot of growing up to do, as with numerous requests for monies the balance was soon depleted in short bursts of materialistic pleasure with nothing of substance to show in the aftermath. Whilst not considered at that stage, grandmother's wise words would come to bear five or six years later. "You can only wear one pair of shoes at a time Philip. You should always put money away for a rainy day." God, it rained nearly every day, which could make me a millionaire.

This was, if I recollect late '68, and two things initially had an impact upon our lives, Katie's and mine.

1st Part

We had come from completely different family structures. Katie's from a deeply (blind faith) Catholic family, her father a coal miner, mother housekeeper and hospital orderly and five siblings (three sisters and two brothers). The girls studied to become teachers, which became their life careers and the two brothers went on to senior management within Scottish Customs and management of a large building supply business. In short, from the extremely low income, they managed to send all children to college or university and still put food on the table. Holidays at best were infrequent visits to St Andrews. It is interesting to note that when we brought Katie's mother out to Australia for her first visit (she did five), it was the first time she had been out of the UK, at 68 years of age. What a world of expectation and presumption that capitalism had contrived.

Katie's father died of black lung/emphysema. His illness, as such brought Katie, Louise and the others together. I was not involved. One daughter with a child and out of wedlock, now another live-in partner to consider and I felt it best to bide my time. This was too much for blind faith, local community and ridicule to expect. That came later, regrettably never to my face. Specifically, in some sections of the community standing opinionated outlaws.

So, I was relegated to the flat, my thoughts and boredom. I re-painted the whole flat. Ian favoured somewhat unusual colours for his private domain and I recollect red walls and purple ceiling, which complemented the blue satin sheets and large volumes of sexual positioning, detailed by various authors. Our clothes, at that point, were army disposal wear, which further enhanced the image of flagellation and bondage. Handed out in bucket loads to his girlfriend who appeared to be an extremely well-read happy individual. She certainly never showed any signs of whip marks. The noise from their room was always one of great laughter and muffled grunts and groans.

A large proportion of our transient flatmates were Jewish Poles. Children of parents who had suffered under the extremes of the Nazis-surviving to pass this instinct to the next generation. Consequently, appreciating the opportunities that they were being given, unlike their parents. In hindsight, I believe that this transitional leaving home procedure, specifically to a university city, allows the youth experimentation in life that can ultimately both mature you early and make one more self-sufficient. Certainly, less inwardly focused and broader in conversational content than much of the youth of today.

I despair at the numerous excuses, and that is all they are, that youth are still living at home with the separated mother who still makes the bed, sorts the clothes, washes and cleans up whilst the lazy blighter never leaves the computer gaming screen – and this is at 25 or 30 years of age. Because they cannot afford to do so. We called it communal living. Parenting has certainly failed, no matter the cost of accommodation. The Chinese, Indians and Japanese get it, get out and look after yourself. They do it. Why not Australians? The principal word, being spoilt. You have to prepare for us, your parents, to be looked after in our older age. Makes sense. The flat painted, the 2nd thing happened. I went back to Middlesbrough for a couple of days.

I decided to pay my regards to Mr and Mrs Walker at the 'Linthorpe Hotel', it was lunch and as I walked into the cocktail bar, the usual business crowd were there. Pink gins, Dubonnet and Gin and Tonic. I was warmly welcomed by all, wanting to know how my studies were progressing and what I was considering after the finals. Was I coming back to the North of England? Unsaid untruths – Never, Ever. This was always an impressive group of business royalty. The head of Dorman Long, soon to become British Steel, a senior regional for Marks and

Spencers, Radio Rentals Director (I always remember him, as the cad was having an affair when in town with a very attractive sales rep, possibly the reason for visitation), Sir and Lady Siller, the Winterschladens and one other man. Always conversing, nonetheless quiet in speech and unassuming. They all drove the top range of motor vehicles whilst his was the basic Morris motor car of the day. These individuals, either for lunch or pre-theatre, were often in formal black tie and cummerbund, gowns, long dress gloves; yet this other man was always plainly dressed in something such as tweed slacks and a casual shirt. I had always noticed this as an employee, specifically as all that he drank was half a pint of bitter, only ever one. As opposed to what then was accepted as leading edge. The top-shelf.

When I arrived home, I asked my father, "Who this man was and why would he be with that particular group?" My father initially showed significant annoyance and I received a reply as such.

"Are you being arrogant son or just stupid? Why shouldn't be there?"

"But Dad he seems so different, they are all wealthy and all he drinks is a half-pint, all he drives is a Morris." What followed was a little lesson in life that, whilst not fully appreciated, became a reality later in my 'growing up', independence and comfort at all levels of society. This was very much a British dialogue that you are no better than others nor are they better than you. Not necessarily true, however, realising later that which he was trying to suggest. However, my father's comment and partial quotes to Kipling, "Walk with the king nor lose the common touch theory, etc." Whatever life projection is not all that it seems. That you should never judge a person's worth by the size of the car, the home or suburb they live in, the clothes they choose to wear, or indeed the food or drink they indulge. A German prefers Kessler and Sauerkraut to an Englishman's roast beef and Yorkshire pudding. A Jew may eat Kosher and an Indian generally favours curry. What matters is that they are all different and must be true to themselves. How they integrate into society and what good they do for others less fortunate. This theme continued for a short period and he finished by saying what I found to be profound, "no matter what is your status Philip, you have to be comfortable in your own skin and true to your beliefs. Do you understand son?"

"Yes, Dad," And incidentally, that man has built and bought businesses that employ many, many people and would realistically have more material wealth than the others, yet comfortable and confident in his own ability, he chooses not to flaunt it.

It could be said that the democratisation of capitalism in the '70s, specifically in America and the Americanised Australia, deployed a theory that 'bigger' and 'more of' was the status of success. The 'wants for' not the 'need for' with consumptive addictions driving purchase for stuff at any cost. Generally, a credit card or extended fixed mortgage, fuelling supply of the scarce resource, deforestation, fossil fuel, pollution and Petrochemical bi-product waste. The need to have it now. An insecure shallow populous.

Whilst with unravelled society and personal discipline decline. Self-importance and actualisation have driven shallow conversations to the fore. While a new pair of shoes, house, car or holiday takes precedence over how your grandmother is unless it's the consideration of her will. We have become a very selfish, self-serving community, extremely uncomfortable in our own skin, nor trust in those around us. Katie and I do not wish to fit into this classification; however, others will judge that. If that makes me perceived as arrogant, well so be it.

Katie arrived back at the flat from her father's funeral to find that I had painted everything, including the piano, white. No doubt McCartney's influence. It had given her the chance to parade 'the baby' to the clan, and, whilst I had not met him at that point, I will always be grateful for the care and attention I know that John Clarkin gave Louise. Others more pious seeing her, Catherine, as a sinner and loose woman, although they never actually had the conviction to say. Not unlike my family. Excepting that, they were straightforward in opinion, as always. Nonetheless only considering one limited opinion for conversation, often wrong.

College time moved closer to exams and I decided that I must consider the future and look for employment opportunities. The Merchant Navy Catering Corp, The Royal Household or Hotel all seemed an opportunity and I was starting to have confidence in my own ability. I was unquestionable competent in both short-order or a la carte. Had a good understanding of front of house and housekeeping, as a result, not truly appreciated past employments and was becoming reasonably competent in administrative inventory, cash flow and accounts. At that period in history a physical procedure of paperwork. I didn't get my first calculator until two years later and whilst Turing had developed the first computing machine in 1936, the thought of a Mac/DOS was not yet understood.

I was fascinated with the composition of food, nonspecific ingredients and enhanced international flavour. However, more attracted as to how much a good cost, the supply chain, the overall costing of ingredient requirement, margins. Linking all other aspects to ensure the ultimate profit of a business. In specific terms-management.

In looking at various employment opportunities the one that fulfilled my objectives of management control and more learning, came from a strange quarter. In hindsight, Katie's pushing in terms as to the thought of long-term security and pension. The Edinburgh Zoo, as Assistant Manager. A promotional opportunity for a young person to oversee the running of the food operations, staff and stock control. A starting salary of some thirteen thousand pounds per annum sealed the desire, and Katie's, and I already envisaged my successful application. Not so, and my first task of unbridled bureaucracy ensued, "doing things the same for years" whilst opportunity, creativity and progress pass you by. I attended three interviews. My background and work experience were, 'exceptional for such a young man' (20 years of age) and once I had also passed my exams in the coming months, I would be a highly sought candidate. When I was older: maybe 23 or 24. God help me, thank the heavens I was not black or female. I would probably progress to toilet cleaner or indeed if the all-male, 55-year-old Scottish board approved, maybe 'muck out the elephant enclosure'.

This set up and influenced, to this day, an intense dislike or patience for public service bureaucracy and autocracy. Unless, without the capitalist structure, they are nimble, adaptive, imaginative. Focused accountability, providing to the government, support and advice that ensures the growth of private businesses, qualify competitive leads and enforcement of specific rules and regulations. Ensuring pro-active quality government whilst minimising corruption and red tape. Very few are now found in democratic regimes ultimately wasting billions in taxation funding, providing substandard service departments with no accountability to K.P.I's, productivity or staff morale. And here we are, men going into space, very soon to the moon and I am four years too young to assist in the running of a zoological food service module. Thank heavens I never succeeded in the application – 'Bureaucracy Killing Democracy'.

Katie and I had a growing intimacy that had much in common; however, my second love was to Louise. She was extremely stubborn, as I was, and maybe this focused my attention. She had been allowed to 'get away with anything', so the 'McLean' teachings of table manners and etiquette, putting toys away and not 'demanding' whilst shopping provided a challenge. On a number of occasions around 24 months old, it was difficult to promote the splade and spoon type of child cutlery. Particularly that the food was meant for the mouth or the bib. A plastic number with a spill base to hold the droppings and not on the floor. In a tantrum, because she refused to eat what was given rather than "mummies" chocolate biscuit. The words were not quite yet correctly stated, the intention was perfectly clear. On one such day, she 'waddled' to the kitchen bench in front of our 3rd-floor window and in an extremely deft movement, the bib was dispatched to the yard below. Somewhat like a Frisbee, not yet discovered. The look of defiance, up to your bum chum, I am in charge here.

I was often at home more than Katie, consequently spending many hours talking, playing and at times questioning. I have no recollection of ever being 'hit by my family'. Although I often received a 'whack' across the ear for some form of typically obnoxious behaviour, generally from my grandmother. I did get the cane, I deserved it and as a believer in 'appropriate discipline', I have no regrets. However, the upbringing was, you do not ever 'hit' women and you do not ever "hit" children, you walk away if your frustration was intense for a particular negative reason. However, one day the tantrums went too far, resulting in a smack to the backside (the only time ever) and I found myself in more personal grief than Louise. Given that she was still in nappies, it was more action than any chance of pain.

I was annoyed and disillusioned because my job application had been rejected until these boring farts deemed me older and how or why I forget, I found myself in the Australian Embassy discussing travel to Australia.

It proceeded extremely quickly in those days (populate or perish was the theme) and, whilst I paid no attention, nor cared, it was still a white-only policy, and yes this is 1969. Myself and college mate Alistair were accepted. The notion being to 'see Australia somehow'. Travel to South America by coastal freighters, hitchhiking into Mexico, through America back to Canada to tell my Uncle George about my exploits. Nothing concerned me to my way of thinking that this was normal. To my family shock horror and Napier College and my qualification. Well, forget that I became a college 'dropout'. It took some time to convince Katie that I would not be very long on this adventure. Extremely somewhat immature thinking when one considers that, if you broke your agreed two-year term with the Australian authorities, all monies were to be repaid. Again, I didn't care, so what, I'm okay. Don't worry about anyone else that cares for you, loves you and is generally concerned for your actions.

Years later my father told me he was in tears when thinking about what I was embarking on, however realised that no matter how irresponsible or immature it may seem he had achieved his objectives: to create an independent young adult and that his tears realised were of pity, for himself. He lost two wives and now he was losing his son forever.

Farewells were said, tears we shed and I committed to writing regularly and that if all went well, I would send for Katie and Louise. So, the next experience and journey began.

A 707 aircraft with various exotic stopovers for refuelling occurred and we arrived in the Great Southern Land, into Darwin. After the stairs were brought to the forward doors, a person walked through the aircraft cabin spraying 'insect exterminate' at everything and everyone. At which point we were allowed to alight the aircraft, being advised to walk through a 'shallow foot bath' of disinfectant positioned on the concourse. The outside temperature was hot and humid, levels of the same that had previously not been experienced nor prepared for, specifically the appropriate type of clothing attire.

The airport gave the impression of an army Nissan hut in 1910, not a major airport. Our destination was Adelaide and therefore after transferring to a smaller aircraft we continued our flight of discovery.

After arriving in Adelaide, we were met by immigration, given an envelope containing general information about Australia, applicable Government and Public Services, accommodation and job-seeking methodology. They took us and others to the West End of Hindley Street in the centre of the city, leaving us at 'a boarding house' whereby we booked in and that was it. I was in a new world, the beer was very, very cold, only two varieties, Westend and Southwark and the food were basic, extremely basic.

I was a Pom and everyone spoke strangely. A good afternoon was g'day mate, 'ow ya doing? Now I know why my grandmother was pleased that I did quite well in my English language and literature O levels, these people obviously had not done so well! I came to understand this as laconic now see it as lazy. I was taught that a kid was an animal and a baby goat, generally part of a herd. That a child was human in species and singular. That children were plural.

The point I make is the lowering of educational standards – far worse today, to (1) appease the needs of inferiority in teaching quality, training and appropriate salary structure (2) the difficulty of integrating multilingual teaching requirements for significant numbers of low socio groups, specifically those from war zones and or ethnic environs where male dominance prevails. Women were often seen as lesser individuals and (3) politicians over the past 50 years who listened to theory – not tried and proven practice. Australia now pays dearly for this laconic excuse. We should have raised the bar not lowered it, our migrant intakes and First nations would have praised us, competent on the world stage with newfound skills. Not as is oft the case causing disruption owing to an inferior education.

We soon found various job offerings, indeed an exceptional opportunity, and within the week, we had all secured employment. Me as a chef. Ex-Oil NL, an Australian Registered American funded mineral exploration company located in remote parts of outback Australia geo-surveying for various types of minerals, copper, gold, ore, diamonds and uranium etc. I was interviewed by Mike Cole a tall gregarious Australian rig tool pusher, a rig boss, in charge of drilling and exploration for bore samples. Peter Walkley, head chef and catering manager sent his apologies, he was detained in Queensland. He had read my CV, references and overview of skills and was very impressed; looking forward to meeting me once, I arrived at Mt Painter Base Camp in the Flinders Ranges South Australia. I was to work 12-hour shifts, two weeks on, two weeks off, paid with a starting wage of $70.00 per week (I believe this was my starting salary if however, I am wrong, it was pretty close. The average wage in Adelaide was approximately $35, I recollect). We flew to Arkaroola Homestead and drove to the base camp.

Now, this all sounds straightforward for a 'pommie bastard'. Once more, my life education is to take a dramatic step forward. The plane: well I now fly massive jets, roads are tarmacadam, one or two lanes each way. A homestead is a farm, generally close to a large town with normal facilities and if you drive to a destination, it's usually relatively close if hitchhiking, a motor vehicle, or so I imagine. Not so Australia's infrastructure in 1969 and the country is vast miles and miles of nothing.

I was to report to the departures desk at Adelaide Airport (a large shed in a paddock) with a kitbag, chef's knives, whites and toiletries. Nothing else was required. Alcohol was forbidden and a dismissible offence, today sadly a memory nonetheless a great practice, both for one's health, safety, relationships and one's wallet. You don't spend any money.

When I arrived however no jet was visible, only a small 4-seater Piper which looked something like my childhood flight with Uncle Paddy at Uxbridge. Paul was the pilot and he has three passengers. One Pom (me), one drunk, Doug, on the way back from leave and one Croatian, Vic Pesic, who was later to be best man at our wedding as Graham R. was held up in Singapore. That's later. We bobbed around in the hot wind currents for a couple of hours, flying over scrub and dessert, until we finally identified a green speck of land surrounded by never-ending red dirt. The green proved to be the garden areas for Arkaroola and the bush airstrip. Just add water and anything will grow in this environment. As anyone who has seen the wildflowers after rain, around Lake Frome or Eyre – it's beautiful. It was hot, about 42C when we arrived. A Toyota Ute, with a front passenger bench seat, arrived to take us to Painter base camp. As I was both the 'rooky and pom', I was designated at the rear of the Ute. The driver, Jock McVicker, a Glaswegian, loud, funny and later, to be extremely supportive of me in my adaption to this different scape. The drunk, Doug – the camp janitor, now almost sober and Vic in the front.

We drove through bulldust, water holes, all on gravel, what they called 'sealed' roads. Sealed, I think they forgot the sealer and only used the dust or gravel, and it was damn hot. As darkness fell, we arrived at a locked gate which just read 'keep out', proceeding on to eventually climb up and down mountain tracks, my not knowing where on earth I was going. Only the next trip on that 'road' to realise that it was basically the width of a D9 dozer blade, cut out of the hillside, no bitumen or Armco here. Just a long drop to the bottom if you got it wrong. We arrived at Painter quite late, dinner had been served and whilst a cook served the new arrivals, Peter walked me around the camp explaining facilities, whilst introducing me to various personnel. He then organised dinner – the largest "T" bone steak I had ever seen, it was half a steer, salad and fries. He was middle-aged, portly, somewhat effeminate (married with children in Brisbane), incredibly funny and ultimately proved a memorable boss, allowing me freedom of decision, supportive and complementary to my achievements. Never claiming credit for anything that I introduced.

The mess hall consisted of a dining area, service point kitchen, preparation, ranges salamander, fryer, fridges, freezer and dry goods storage and pantry. All units were demountable, the power provided by a huge diesel generator that operated 24/7 and the water supply was a bore. It was a different world from anything that I could have imagined. In the coming weeks, I got to know Peter and it was obvious that he respected what skills I had, specifically menu, French and choices optional to that which was presently served. Little did I realise that in approximately eight or nine weeks I was to be designated the preparation in the menu and subsequent planning to cook for the S.A. Governor. A specific visit to preview uranium leases, water reserve opportunities and discuss the future of Australia as a uranium nation.

It is interesting to note, as a non-nuclear power, that this particular area, whilst not the richest ore body, indeed proved to be the largest in the world. We sold the stuff but did not use it, leaving the waste for someone else to clean up. Somewhat hypercritical one might suggest. Nothing eventuated with the artesian water options. This was my first insight within Australia into insular, indecisive, extremely conservative thinking by a continent not sure about its own identity. Nor its traditional inhabitants, the Aboriginal. They still have no treaty and we still debate uranium – no real policy on either.

This was 1969, and they, the Aborigines, basically had no rights however, those that I met: roustabout cattlemen and family, I found to be extremely friendly, skilled in their work albeit subservient, something the whites had created. Incredible in their natural tracking skills and knowledge of land and survival skills in a dry inhospitable landscape.

Sometime later in my learning curve, a tracker showed me how to find water and basic survival food source in the semi-desert/scrub environs of this region. Something, as a natural skill, was clearly passed down from generation to generation as to specific areas, nonetheless at one with the land.

Those that I met, more specifically women, had a good command of English and generation education. I assumed as a result of Missionary education and what we now know as 'the Stolen Generation'. As wrong as their treatment had been, something definitely became worse for them with the introduction of supposed equality and welfare. One contemplates as to why these "elders" did not pass on these English skills to the next generations in the 80s and 90s. With certain aspects of their rights appearing in many ways to go backwards. Whilst I am not convinced that the principles of capitalism are being correctly applied to them (greed, power and corruption) there is no question that if your main educated language is specific to the nationality i.e. Japan – Japanese, Indonesia – Indonesian and so on. Thus, irrespective of past colonial beliefs, you are better served being taught that main language first and your particular dialogue most definitely, when the main language has been learnt for your survival, in the real world. Irrespective of agreement or not, one could suggest that in recent years countries like Germany, Japan, China who, after their main language taught English as a secondary, developed greater capitalistic opportunity in a 'free trade' global economy.

I do not disagree that one must maintain one's identity and heritage. However, rightly or wrongly, in the case of Australia, the main language is English. You are further jeopardising your children's future if their main language is location dialect. If one looks at the elders of today, many from the stolen generation, their position and respect are secured by their command of the English language. If I were them, I would be demanding command of English first then most definitely their indigenous language in equal competence second. As we now see in China enabling competitive movement on the world stage. I know that on business in Japan I always felt 'humbled' in that my business colleagues' hosts spoke fluent English (Harvard education in one instance) and I did not speak Japanese. Maybe a throw away from the arrogant colonial era, whereby the British expected the other party to learn, not so them. Not unlike teaching French and German when that is pure history.

Work progressed extremely well; I was accepted and respected by my immediate work colleagues, geologists, drillers, head office and the like. Peter and I worked while he was in camp, extremely well. Our systems and organisational workflow were extremely compatible (we, despite his girth were both extremely quick workers) and I enjoyed the 'free Aussie banter', non-class distinctive as with the UK. It did not matter which school you went to, how you dressed or spoke, until you passed comment, perceived still to this day, as a critical judgement of Australia. Australians are in many instances regrettably unable to accept criticism and as such are not prepared to accept failings. My belief, if you do not wish to accept a possibility or alternative, you are hardly likely to make a change, subsequently restricting the opportunities to yourself or your country. If you are not adapting, you are actually going backwards.

Whilst I did not appreciate my life at that point in time. To an Aussie, not travelled, had possibly limited exposure to employment, no student living ethos and living in a city (Adelaide) that certainly was not cosmopolitan, more like a big country town and an extremely conservative male chauvinistic dominated workforce (the females had terminated employment when married) and a community totally focused to church, I was actually quite 'worldly'.

The Australian dialogue 'go back to where you came from' was and always has been a common theme within Australia. If you try to challenge the status quo, constructively critiquing suggestions for considered change, you fall foul of ostracisation. I was hearing critical comments as to wog, pommie bastard, dago and the like, however, my turn soon came.

I had become particularly friendly with Graham Reynolds, a dinky-di well-educated Australian who had welcomed me into his home on our weeks off, introducing me to various friends. He and others would often ask questions as to what other countries and their peoples were like. What was London like, how cold was Montreal and did St Laurance actually freeze? Simple stuff and I would comply. The inevitable question was asked, which not intentionally meant, was seen as a criticism of Australia, its shallow view and in my opinion, generally portrays insecurity in one's own demeanour (Trump being a recent case). However, never one to shy away from an argument, I looked for an answer that would not end the friendship. Intending to create the medium and attitude as to how Graham (everyone is different) would see me differently. Not critical comparison, merely that there are many alternatives in life and that we must always maintain an open mind if we are to be constantly moving forward.

So, my response was somewhat like this: – "Mr Reynolds, when you have worked and lived in Croatia, Kuwait, Bahrain, Singapore and Australia, as has Vic. He is not the wog. Or Holland, Belgium, Canada, Scotland (slightly gilding the lily) as I have, then you will be worthy of entertaining discussion. Until then, "I would suggest you shut up as you have no idea of what you are talking about." At which stage I walked out. Something presumably worked, as from then on, I was the 'Englishman' and Vic was no longer 'the Wog'.

Whilst Australians are now well-travelled, very little has changed and I find it both annoying and disappointing that these views still prevail today. I have always maintained that if you cannot accept or give constructive comments and critiques then you are denying yourself imagination to many alternative possibilities or actions. Australians cannot to this day accept and generally only criticise 'in the pub' or facial twitter. Very sad. We are a lesser community for this failure. Our youth are unable to stand up to their own personality bullying.

I was missing Katie and Louise immensely. There was no shortage of women in Adelaide, however, I was not interested. I was sure this was not a reaction to distance, loneliness or heaven forbid, self-pity. I was convinced that she was the right person and as we wrote almost daily, letters to each other, I decided to send my mother's wedding ring (which my father had given to me some years earlier) as a gesture of long-term intention. The response was yes and incidentally, in 50 years, the ring has not been taken off, and she organised her and Louise's transportation. We cannot remember if she 'came as a migrant 10-pound pom or we paid' however, the trip was scheduled for late January 1970.

At the time of this news, and as I told you earlier, I have always been blessed, always "falling on my feet", in all aspects of life. Peter asked me to go to New Guinea and consolidate the camp on Manus Island. The basics were in place, however freezers and supplies from Brisbane were yet to arrive. I jumped at the opportunity, not to mention the $350 tax-free remote location weekly wage. It was heaven-sent. Nowhere to spend it, a good thing as grandmothers' frugal teachings had not sunk in yet (and didn't till my mid 20's) although I was starting to amass a 'reasonable' bank account status.

I flew to Brisbane, said hello to everyone, Peter briefed me regards the business and a couple of days later I flew to Moresby with Chick Barret and Stuart Simpson. From there, I think we flew DC3 aircraft to the navy base and then the company speed boat around the coast to the camp.

Strange, as to recent years and what Manus Island is known, for now, refugees. However, in late '69 it was, had been one of the main naval bases and airstrip for the Japanese and allied/Anzac Forces of WWII. Flying over the lagoon, so crystal clear, one could see the outline of planes, battlecruisers and anything else that had been destroyed. No doubt the hundreds of innocent service personnel who sacrificed their lives for their country. The Exoil Petromin camp was located opposite a pristine beach, beautiful blue water, in a cleared jungle area. The accommodation and mess facility were initially locally built wood and (I think) banana leaf thatch and wall, ceiling fans and minimalistic furniture. To a 21-year-old (just) Brit it was picture book stuff, it was paradise and this was work. Half your luck Phil, who could ever have imagined. No pollution, that would come later, coconuts, bananas and bucket loads of fresh fish on the doorstep. I was in heaven.

To anyone of a younger generation and more concerned about deforestation, land degradation, Colonial and American thinking, I would skip the next section.

The Americans were building (trying to) a road that would facilitate land rig movement to geo sample site drill holes. The choice of road base material was coral. Yes, correct. Coral ripped out of the pristine shoreline and trucked to the construction zone. A D9 bulldozer with chains ripped the forest habitat to shreds. The monsoon rains came daily, on the dot late afternoon. Consequently, 50% of work completed that day was 'washed away' due to the exposed red mud clay under the surface with no root growth left nor canopy restraint to soften the downpour. A mini Amazon disaster. The half-mile road had already cost some $250,000.00, great ingenuity! 50 years ago, and we have still not learned.

Food ingredients. Well, I was no better. Our main supplies had not arrived by barge from Brisbane, so what do you do, you improvise, Veau Tomate, Cochin de lait, Homard. We had a wonderful fresh larder on our doorstep. Send the boys out for a couple of turtles, you had your veal, no one knew the difference. 20c a catch, Cochin de lait, wild young piglet 30c. Homard, the local and plentiful lobster, 5c. As much fish as you wanted and local fresh vegetables and seasonal fruit from the village market and you had your menu. Imagine today, I would be locked up for life. Turtles, wild pig, the first nations did it daily, subsistence farming, why shouldn't we?

Katie's letters arrived fortnightly in one large bundle and presumably mine in response to her, this provided an evening of enjoyable reading, finding out what was happening, how all the flatmates were, how work was going. And of course, my little girl. Now at times quite naughty as she no longer had Phil to organise her tantrums. I was pleased that I was no longer 'Pill'. The planning of travel was well organised and they would arrive late January 1970 via Perth on the new Boeing 747 aircraft. So, what do I do over Christmas? Why not stay on Manus and let others have a break and then take time out for Katie and Louise's arrival.

With the New Guinea schedule, unlike Painter, we worked five weeks on and two weeks paid leave, off. Today it seems quite a long time, however, the time seemed to evaporate and I, therefore, saw no problem in spending 10 weeks in paradise. It would most definitely enhance the bank account. I needed to secure tenancy in Adelaide, a car for Katie and crockery, cutlery, bedding etc. So, this was the opportunity to consolidate resources.

I fail to mention that the multi-national mix of skilled employees were supported in menial, unskilled labour requirement by around 100 locals. They were managed by Doug, previously a public service Kiep officer, who worked for many years in PNG, He spoke fluent pigeon, understanding the various dialects, regional, tribal customs and beliefs. Colonial living in the 50s and 60s centred around the club. Not unlike the officer mess mentality and of course this involved alcohol. In Doug's case, too much, and he subsequently became an alcoholic. He left PNG to "sort himself out" securing the janitorial position at Painter, irrelevant to his capability. Knowing that the company was alcohol-free, one has to respect that mindset given his particular demon. When management realised his skills, he was asked to go back to Manus Island, appreciating that alcohol was not available.

Those exposed to the Colonial lifestyle living availability of such locations as Singapore or Hong Kong during these years would appreciate my comments, hopefully, that the slave-like conditions no longer exist. Doug's responsibility was overseeing the daily routine for the various camp department requirements. In my case, mess hall, kitchen and accommodation. For others mechanical, drills and supply. He was extremely well respected by the locals and it saddened me to see his lifestyle change when on leave and influenced by alcohol, unable to drink moderately.

The local people were 'childlike in demeanour' limited in white man's ways, naive to global realities, however most importantly proud and trusting. Again, taken advantage of by the whites, an all too common occurrence. As a warrior nation, something the Australian Aborigine had not been, they portrayed incredible regional practice and dress. I have always believed that one's true history is represented in both live drawings of both body form, dress and then later photography in historical reference. They projected slim, fit and adaptive bodies to their climate and landscape and lifestyle. Both men and women could comfortably carry loads over a great distance without stopping, whilst the white man required rest regularly in the oppressive humid heat. Doug had boxes and boxes of photographs that he had taken since the 1930s and they portrayed the superb warrior dress and weaponry, not unlike what I imagined the Zulu warrior of the 18th century to have been. Now a decimated people, forged in welfare, corruption and dictatorship. The Papuans practised what is called 'payback'.

That is, if a member of their tribe was to be killed, accidentally or by intent: a life had to be taken from the offending tribe. Plus, witchcraft, which I believe to be active in the Highlands today. To this, we brought Seiko watches, transistors, Elvis movies, money, hypocrisy and white man's arrogance.

American drillers and tool pushers could earn as much as $600 per week. The indigenous wage was $10 per week. A block of soap, a stick of tobacco, newspaper for creating the cigarette, (Aunt Nan would have loved this place) salt, sugar, tinned meat and a towel. Modern-day slavery, a living wage, what bullshit. What we see today as with aborigines and other first peoples, is a welfare mentality, capitalist corruption by the government and senior facilitators waste of scarce resources. Most importantly loss of tradition and pride.

Why did we have to drag them into the 20th century, unprepared and then leave them to suffer and struggle in the 21st?

I stayed over Christmas and yet again, another seminal moment occurred. Myself, and a few others (including Jock McVicker), were invited to travel: speedboat, canoe and then walk through the jungle to the tribal village of Michael Somare (later to enter Parliament, subsequently becoming Prime Minister twice) to live and experience life in New Guinea. My accommodation was (an honour, I later found) to be an important hut, on stilts with grandparents residing below – in this case, the skeletal bodies on wooden frames, bringing good fortune, hunting prowess to those residing above. It certainly was not like this in Middlesbrough; no doubt, grandmother would have been impressed and not forgotten.

We were invited to stay for a number of days and of course, Christmas was not a known entity. Hunting and fishing were organised to facilitate the 'guests'. A group of warriors were dispatched to hunt wild boar (pig) and all the women prepared vegetables and fish wrapped in leaf in preparation for something that resembled a New Zealand Hangi ceremony. A pig arrived, skewered and tied to a pole carried by two men and proudly paraded around the guests. Alive, Stone Age transportation logistics. That night we enjoyed the feast, which in this case consisted of pork, ripped from one leg only. It was some hours later that I found the pig, tethered near a hut, this time with only three legs. They removed the fourth leg area covered in something that looked like tree sap. Whoa! Well if you don't have a fridge what do you do to keep it fresh, improvise. I did not eat pork for quite some time, obviously few traditional Jews residing in PNG.

The next day the males retreated to prepare themselves for a tribal show of strength. The spectacle was fantastic, headdress of beautiful bird feather plumage, exotic colours and ochre facial masks. We had been advised, correctly or not, that cannibalism had existed into the 1930s. To be confronted by 150 menacing warriors poking spear or arrow close to your nose was a 'let's say an exhilarating moment'. To be honest, "Bloody terrifying for a short period." Until one realised this show was out of respect. We discovered later that we were seen as being 'Ime good fella good boss. Ime looks after little fella good, plenty food and Bako'. Maybe had they not thought so, we may have disappeared, into a large pot! Herbs, spices and boiling water.

Time soon passed and I flew back to Brisbane. De-briefed Peter and headed for Adelaide, to wait for Katie and Louise.

Kathy, our highly competent administrative lady in the Adelaide office had overseen the lease and tenancy agreement for me whilst in New Guinea. So, all I had to do was acquire the basics and move in. They, the flats were the very latest in Adelaide, fully furnished and called the Spanish flats, on Anzac Highway. Still there today, 50 years later and they still look good. In 1970, they were leading edge.

I bought a car for Katie who was yet to learn to drive. A little blue Morris 1100 for $1100, and was promptly to be told by Reynolds "I was a stupid bastard as I had been ripped off and why had I not spoken to him?" My first purchase of substance, you could buy a house for $7-8 thousand and I muffed it. I never made the mistake again in car nor house.

It was extremely hot weather, mid to high 30's. I was as brown as a berry and adapted to the heat very easily. Katie and Louise arrived, however, tired they soon settled into a welcome party with my newfound friends, who by now knew more about Katie and Louise than her family. Katie loved the apartment, warmth and Adelaide. We bought what we required with many excursions to the shops, all paid for with our savings, only what we required. No credit in those days.

Grandmother's sentiment was starting to bite, "only ever buy what you can afford, do not get into debt Philip."

"Yes Gran," we visited various South Australian tourist places, spending a few days in the Barossa Valley, its German heritage and wineries. We visited the beach at Glenelg, Katie had never seen sand like this (only pebbles at St Andrews) and warm water. I bought Louise what Australians called floaties, a buoyancy device that kept the head up and arms out so the child could paddle.

Gaining confidence in the water, wet eyes or not, she took to it like a duck to water, Katie more like a skinny hippopotamus. I was quite a good swimmer and having taught Louise the basic strokes we later sent her to professional swimming lessons, consequently becoming extremely competent by the age of six or seven, winning many medals in swimming for school and State. She also beat a young girl who ended up swimming in the Olympics. Not so her dear mother, who, sadly for many years became the butt of our jokes. There is nothing more hilarious than a six or seven-year-old trying to teach her mother appropriate breathing, stroke and leg movement. All in one sequence whilst the trainee, her mother, has trouble doing one thing at a time, extremely difficult. So, it was more gulps, swallow, flounder and cough than an annoyance. Comment: "I'm not doing this anymore, Louise."

The time came for me to start thinking about going back to work at Painter for two weeks and so we decided to spend the afternoon at the beach on day one, more for day two and fly out on day three.

As I said I was extremely brown, Katie was, 'lily-white with Scottish/Irish skin pigmentation' and no amount of warning could permit common sense and cover-up, what later became known as slip, slop, slap. Consequently, arriving home brighter than a red traffic signal, dehydrated, forming blisters and nausea creating a need to drive to the hospital and 'a very long' hot night. The next day staying in bed and the third day, my leaving.

A neighbour's daughter, Cathy (they had secured employment as the manager/caretakers) insisted that she would take care of Katie and of course, nurse Mc Lean. Louise, not yet three, "I will look after my mummy and make her better." Still brings tears to the eyes.

When I got back to the camp, Peter asked me to send a cook over to Paralana hot springs camp, to relieve the cook, George Stone, a wonderful old man full of "tall stories", bush cook, truck driver, shearer, roustabout, you name it, George had done it, I had never seen his kitchen nor his cooking, so I decided to go myself.

Reynolds passed some comments like, "Thank God for that, we might now get a decent meal out there." I paid little attention, I was given the water truck as my transport and followed Graham on his drive to Paralana and on to the rig site so that I didn't get lost in the scrub as a stupid bloody Englishman usually did.

What did I find? Nothing like I could have imagined. Old timber and aluminium two-berth caravans, Franklins, I think. No air conditioning, toilet or shower cabin. The toilet was an old twenty-gallon oil drum with a hole cut into both ends, a toilet seat attached one end, the other placed over a 20-foot borehole. Out in the scrub, not quite our old campsite in Whitby, more like Nanas, with a long drop. Showers, just jump into the hot springs with a bar of soap.

The kitchen was to one end of a stripped-out caravan with a bench, breakfast-style eating to the other end. Flies everywhere and to this day the vision encountered will never disappear. Old George, ready to be picked up by Arkaroola Homestead transport, standing next to a domestic gas cooktop and oven. He was dressed in slacks, shirt and trilby hat, a little pipe in his mouth, alight, his port (case) was on the floor ready to 'get going now' whilst preparing food for the boys.

The food, heaven forbid, was lambs brains simmered in milk. He welcomed me and sneezed. At which point copious quantities of pipe ash entered the pot and, to my amazement, he kept stirring. He bade farewell and left; I never saw him again, maybe my doing? Painter and New Guinea were spotless, Peter's standards were exceptional. Consequently, how old George had managed to get away with these conditions, I will never know. I never asked. I just rolled up my sleeves and in the next four hours endeavoured to clean the place as best could be achieved before dinner service.

I threw the brains out, cleared the fridges (gas), dispatching most of the food which was either maggot blown or rotten to the rubbish pile. Somehow, I salvaged enough ingredients to create a decent dinner for the guys when they arrived off shift and breakfast/crib for the next day. It must have been acceptable because all I heard was, "That's the best bloody tucker we have ever eaten at Paralana." That night I got on the two way and radioed for a stock delivery of decent ingredients, a cook, John Noble and lots of cleaning goods. When John arrived, we sorted the place out and agreed on an appropriate menu of meat, fish and salads relevant to the size of the kitchen/storage capacity. I left a very happy group of workers and drove back to Painter unaided. Consistent with the camp facilities (they were paid extra) now that they had good food and hygiene.

The primary reason for this story is to briefly depict the growth of a young boy into adulthood, his life with one woman and ultimately being told late in life that he had an inoperable rare cancer, Metastatic carcinoma. Whilst at the same time a double whammy occurs and that woman, Katie, is diagnosed with Dementia, later confirmed as Alzheimer's.

I make note that, whilst not interested in trying to prove my theory, (more focused on caring for Katie and survival); I believe that this period in life's cycle is the potential reason for my cancer. Indeed, possibly a reason for certain health outcomes of first peoples and general inhabitants in remote country regions. That is, mineral-laced (uranium) bore water. As my diagnosis is termed a slow cancer, not unlike the longer-term effect and outcome of radiation poisoning, asbestosis, coal dust and indeed cigarette smoking, to name a few. Chernobyl, Maralinga and Fukushima.

To my point. Drinking water that came from various boreholes, dispersed around the area and all drawn and drank unfiltered from rich ore body country, specifically uranium ore bodies. We were also all continually exposed to the vast mounds of ore samples stored around the Painter location perimeter that the geo team analysed.

The condition, once diagnosed, proved to be extremely rare and in simple terms classified as Neuroendocrine Tumours, in my case, inoperable metastatic carcinoid syndrome. More of that later.

Our life in Adelaide was tremendous. However, I believed that moving to a different environment, a three-year-old for basic company, no gainful employment and Katie was bored and lonely whilst I was away. Therefore, with a suggestion from Cathy, they applied for a job, a sewing machine shop, not selling them but using them, it was an Aussie sweatshop. I appreciated her intentions, not the position. Suggesting that she look for something more appropriate to her training and employment background, she resigned and commenced searching for something more appropriate to her previous skill capacity. John Martins Department Store Group was looking for an administrative assistant/trainee credit supervisor in its Adelaide Head Office, Rundle Street Store and she applied. John Martins was a household name in Adelaide, trusted, value, wide product range and reported as a good company to work for. This proved to be correct. She was successful in her application and for the next thirteen years, developed significant skills in office management, customer service and credit management. She ultimately became an Associate Member of the Australian Credit Institute and JP. It was those days when credit was restricted to an appropriate level, realistically determined as to payment capacity. Look out for anyone that became 'stretched' as to payment. If credit officers could not secure terms, "Give it to Katie, she will fix it." Our jobs continued with much enjoyment and we started to see a long-term secure future.

Still not listening to either my grandmother or father's wise words, I continued to "waste monies" still believing that outwardly material possessions mattered. Not so Katie, she more and more commanded control of our finances and quietly our resources grew. We had moved first into a less expensive garden apartment and then to a small basic unit. In the suburb of Plympton with the Reynolds. Maggie was pregnant and both couples saving like hell to buy a house in the Adelaide Hills. They ultimately built in the Coromandel Valley and we bought a renovation job on a very large block in a rural setting, Hawthorndene, 15 minutes' drive from Adelaide, that was later.

On one particular work period, I left Painter, flew home for only a couple of days, flew to Manus Island, staying longer than usual, then on to Perth, Newman and then a specific remote location camp that I forget the name of. It was on the Newman ore train line route.

Life took another turn at this point (a) regular letters were suggesting that when I finally arrived home I should be thinking about coming home for one reason – our wedding, otherwise she may be going back to Scotland and (b) that it may be prudent to seek employment in Adelaide, thereby helping with Louise's upbringing etc, etc. A suggestive, non-negotiable directive.

As I flew into Newman there had been a terrible hurricane, which devastated the West Coast and to say that the flight was terrifying would be an understatement. The plane was a mess when we landed, stuff was thrown around the cabin and I felt physically awful. I assumed it was the flight, big sook, and carried on to find my 'small plane' transport to the camp. An old two-seater bush example with canvas window flaps and the weather was still gale force. It did however have an engine. Considering the vintage, I envisaged rubber band propulsion. Irrespective, we took off, landed in a flooded paddock – somehow and proceeded by 4-wheel drive to the camp. I don't remember the drive to get there or the next two days. I had contracted Malaria and was apparently whisked off to the sickbay, thinking that I was drunk and then realising the reason for my strange mannerism; I was bedridden for some time. I regained my health and flew back to Adelaide and prepared for matrimony and real commitment, till death do us part. I stopped running and so it came to be.

3) Commitment, Coles and Kentucky

I searched for local employment options that would offer exposure to retail management theory, training and opportunity, subsequently choosing G.J. Coles Pty. Australia's nationally respected retailer, known for its exceptional training and promotional opportunity. I told Peter of my intentions, he understood and had indeed expected the choice to come sooner. I was accepted by G.J Coles to work in an A grade store, Rundle Street, Adelaide. Starting my new career in retailing, never to wear the chef's hat again, and a weekly wage of $60.85. I had been earning $350.00!

Katie was earning $35.00 per week, the average wage, we had savings and our respective promotion was our objective, Louise's future schooling and enjoying life.

My learning curve was steep and most enjoyable. I once more realised, irrespective of my irresponsible teens that "the total sum of the parts" may actually amount to something. As usual, I worked hard, focusing on customer service standards and in particular stock control, layup and what was then termed as 'footage'. Later to become known as planograms, schematics or sales product mix, depending on which group you worked for. In very simple terms, the approximate quantity of stock in the correct location at the applicable price point.

In those days (1971) we had to manually work through the process (no word processors, calculators, computers) compiling a historical data file in what was called a footage book. Subsequently physically 'cutting' the goods into the counters and or fixtures. Our primary 'iPhone' of that period was: footage book, pencil, glasscutter, tape measure and your brain. Basically, the objective was to determine what quantity of stock was required in a given space, to return the optimum applicable sales and margin. I received promotions quickly and was promoted to A Grade Department Manager in charge of the ground floor, Rundle Street.

Once more, a turn of events, self-inflicted, changed my direction in life, continuing my dissatisfaction with bureaucracy and autocracy then, as today the greatest roadblock to imagination, creativity, development, moral and business success within both private and public business structures. In my opinion, dramatically affecting the practicality of democratisation. I am not for one moment suggesting that we should rid ourselves of the public system, more the redistribution and appropriate use of funds to the coalface. Better funded teachers and nurses, with more accountability for their actions, reducing back of house duplication and indecision for example, whilst containing budget blowouts through poor productivity outcomes.

As I stated, G.J. Coles – later to become Coles/Myer and now Coles Supermarkets, was an excepted training operative, however, constrained by British style management conservatism.

Your career progression depended on results, how you interacted with your boss (Mr) and was determined by your gender and age as to promotion. You worked at the A Grade Department (as I was), and then D Grade (very small) store as management, progressing up through the grades until you reached A, if you were chosen in the rigorous old boy's club. I thought that I had left that all behind, clearly not so. Consequently, by way of example, an A Grade Assistant Store Manager was in his own right, a manager having worked through all other grades.

No ability to change the system, that's it. No matter how capable you have proven to be you must await your turn, I asked Mr Burdett, the Store Manager, if I could be considered for a country posting (you were allocated accommodation similar to the bank manager of the day, with good community standing) his response sealed my fate. "You have made exceptional progress Philip and you have a very good future with Coles; however, you will have to be a little more patient for a few years yet, you are still very young. This was like the Edinburgh Zoo catering position all over again, at this rate I would be Managing Director at 65 and dead at 67. Not me."

I had heard through a retail business association, that a group of young Canadians were opening chicken outlets in various states. The terminology was fast food operations. Lapointe, Tomlinson, Wales, Wachna and Cowin. In the case of South Australia, Robert (Bob) Lapointe had secured the South Australian franchise for Kentucky Fried Chicken. Cowin for Western Australia. On the way home from work I drove past their office on Greenhill Road, it was getting late, the lights were on and I was welcomed in by Bob (Lapointe). I told him briefly about the situation. We talked for some time about my CV and previous experiences and it was an extremely relaxed informal straightforward discussion. I liked his manner and style, notwithstanding his quite obvious business acumen. He asked me to come in the following evening with the appropriate CV history and advised that I would have an interview with his Operations General Manager, Tom Tomlinson and possibly one of the Area Managers; Graham Collins or Paul Kenny. It was an inspirational interview, informal, open and informative as to both future plans and opportunities for those persons who were prepared to work hard, learn, continue study and thereby enable the development of others relatively quickly. As such, those great plans were being considered for the group, AustCan Foods. I secured the position, six weeks in the Training Store, then a posting to store as Assistant Manager. Starting salary $75.00 per week on a five-day rotational seven-day roster. Tom asked me when I could start and rather cautiously, I said that I wished to show loyalty to G.J. Coles as: "You never know when you may wish to go back as General Manager." This was indeed the first time that I started to take things responsibly and they were, as I discovered later, impressed with my 'maturity and thought process'. I resigned the next day and worked out my four weeks with G.J. Coles. Incidentally, in 1983 I returned to Coles/Myer as Company Merchandising Manager, Food Group Grace Bros. Not quite General Manager nonetheless a senior executive position.

    Katie was happy, Louise was happy and I was ecstatic. Australia was a different world of opportunity. I quickly progressed to Assistant, then Manager of a lower volume operation. The business in those days was Manager, 2 assistant managers, 1 hostess and 15 to 20 casual or part-time employees. I then moved to a higher volume operation and subsequently more staff, sales and profit responsibility.

    Whilst the executive group were Canadians, the franchise was American, so I started to devour any literature on the subject of franchising that I could find. Also, any information regards American corporate business culture, financial planning, and management development. It was there for the offering for those that wanted to 'put in the hard yards'. Whatever store I operated, I lifted sales, profit and started to be heard in management group meetings and seminars.

    One day when visiting head office and about to leave, Tom T (for whom I developed a huge respect, indeed he became one of my foremost mentors as "to getting it right") came out of the office. The comment, "I want to see you, come in." Christ, what had I done? Subsequently, into his office, "How are you doing?"

"Excellent, what's wrong?"

"Relax, don't look so worried, I'm going to promote you to Supervisor reporting directly to Graham Collins (who was my Area Manager) and you will get a motor car."

"Wow, thanks Tom this is fantastic."

"I haven't finished yet, now come into Bob's office."

"Hi Phil, how's things going?"

"Great Bob, thanks for the promotion."

"As Tom would have told you, we are extremely pleased with your work ethic, the way you develop your people and we would like you to be involved in a consulting study with a large international group. I recollect that it was Horwarth and Horwarth. You will be working with Michael Baker who has also been selected from Pizza Palace Restaurant. Incidentally, as your operational financials have been excellent it was appropriate that you participate in this project, which will study better operational and financial opportunities for the group."

Tom then advised that I would now be part of the weekly senior management group briefings, people's discussion, profit and operational issues. Thereby starting my career, which in itself, would fill three volumes of literature. I ultimately became State Manager KFC, South Australia and then what followed were various executive positions at State and General Manager of Major Brand Operations and Consultant, all within multi-site, multimillion-dollar large workforce environs of Branded food and retail.

However, this story is of love, patience, persistence, incompetence and incontinence. Consequently, we will now focus on our respective retirements, ultimate boredom, small business purchase and illness.

We had enjoyed relative success, whatever that is, motivated and extremely lucky to work with some tremendous individuals, making great friends and still feel privileged to have been given the opportunities that we both enjoyed. Would we have been as lucky had we chosen to stay in the UK? I believe so. Ensuring your own success by seeking out opportunity, never giving in to pressure, irrespective as to roadblocks that life situations throw at you. If the side road is failing you, jump onto the freeway and speed up.

In terms of Katie's health, I need to take the reader back briefly to her childhood and what cards were dealt, ultimately enhancing health parameters that have regrettably created her health position today, Alzheimer's.

I would also add, that from a lifestyle standpoint, she has always been slim, active, eating in moderation. Considering my career choices, she has eaten very limited takeaway content up to her 50's, at which point in time she commenced a quite rigid diet of light-limited meat, vegetables, fruit and no 'sugary' products. She smoked until aged 30 years old, finally stopping when I decided that I personally wished to live a healthy lifestyle, preferring that to death at 60 and, whilst enjoying an alcoholic drink, she has always drunk in moderation. She has never taken illegal substances and does not gamble. We dislike consumptive addiction and a weak retail therapy mindset, having always lived a comfortable, yet a frugal lifestyle. Consequently, in all aspects of our activity, we have tried to moderate our waste footprint on the planet, having been intentionally extremely soft-footed. We, therefore, reject the suggestion that we fit the Australian stereotypical baby boomer mindset. A well-quoted phrase, "One eats to live, not live to eat." Sadly, that is not the mindset of many.

Katie contracted rheumatic fever and then later polio, as a child. She recovered from both with no visible signs of disability. Her mother, a devout Catholic, was convinced that it was divine intervention. I believe that advances in medication played a significant role. However, as a medical practitioner will tell you, those persons born in the early 1940s who experienced rheumatic fever, will ultimately have some form of heart malfunction, irrespective of lifestyle. It is basically an undiagnosed time bomb, until it is too late, often resulting in a stroke.

When Katie and Louise arrived in Adelaide, there was no question as to children. We planned, dependant on the financial ability to afford them a good education, two more. After a number of years, however, numerous miscarriages/operational procedures, it was clear that Louise was to be our only child, unless we adopted. Louise at this stage was approximately five and as life cycles prevailed, and the option for adoption, rightly or wrongly, was forgotten.

Consequently, in her late 20's, Katie commenced heart rhythm complications. The calling for various scans leading to the identification of the specific health diagnosis. I would note that much to our deep sadness, Louise encountered period pain issues in her teens followed by general gynaecological problems, finally diagnosed with endometriosis. Maybe genes, maybe hereditary, we will never know as she never wanted to fully discuss the subject with her mother or me, suffering alone.

Katie had insisted that we should have private health insurance both for associated specialist costs and practitioner preference. Canada in many ways was similar to Australia (very close dollar, GDP etc) and I had a vague memory of my cousin Jennifer requiring teeth braces as a child, Grandmother informing me that they had cost an awful lot of money. That sealed the deal and to this day, we have always had private health cover. No matter what the small sacrifice, a few less beers or coffee, no gambling and any Australian (I am sorry to say and make no apologies) is a fool if they don't sacrifice a little to pay for this security and choice, specifically, whilst in gainful employment. Believed invincible in our early years, and with the social community of today, those not privately covered will pay dearly as health issues kick in with middle age and the public health safety net systems becoming overburdened and failing, as they are now with the respective social and financial outcomes, I am convinced that part of our personal ability to access new medical breakthroughs, more skilled and specialist practitioners has been because of private insurance. Not to mention operational cost, new age medication and ongoing instant care options. As I do not believe in the fundamental nature of the charitable protocol, I certainly do not believe in the self-pitying adoption of crowdfunding. More of this corruptive subject later. Not least to say we as a nation are wallowing in melodrama and self-pity.

Specialist visits followed and the diagnosis identified mitral stenosis, eventuating in open-heart surgery and valve repair being required. That, as the valve opened and closed more restrictively, breathing and other issues would eventuate not to mention stroke and of course, one thing not considered nor understood. That is, as the opening and closing action of the valve reduced, so too did the quantity of blood and oxygen being pumped to the brain. Less oxygen to the brain and in an otherwise healthy person, could this be the ticking time bomb for Dementia/Alzheimer's related illness?

I have discussed this with many skilled persons and no one has said no to my theory, that it could be part of the problem. More so, at this stage that we just do not know, it may be a number of critical incidents that result in Dementia.

I would at this stage of dialogue make a statement that you will hear on numerous occasions. It appertains to a significant demographic of the Australian population that indulge in excess of various consumptive wants. The cost that they bring to bear will ultimately become unsustainable and unless politicians have the determination and "guts" to make a radical change, this grouping will have a massive influence on the social fabric of this continent. I would suggest that America, Australia (and its Americanisation) and to a lesser extent the United Kingdom have similar problems. I have developed what I call my (50/50 Rule), based on statistics over the past 50 years. We see obvious and alarming data that now place-specific social trending at, in all cases, more than 50% of the population, increasing each decade over the past 50 years.

The following is an alarming series of well-documented and recorded statistics:

- 50%   Grossly overweight
- 50%   Consuming alcohol regularly at dangerous levels
- 50%   Oversupplied and dependant on prescription medication.
- 50%   Taking illegal drugs
- 50%   Addicted to various forms of gambling
- 50%   Likely to resort to domestic violence
- 50%   Unable to maintain a meaningful and lasting relationship.

Appendix 1 – Hunt/Deakin Letters

You will hear the (50/50 Rule) mentioned numerous times. However, I do stress that this country still has wonderful opportunities. If only our politicians of all parties, could come together for the good of the community and not those with vested interest and subsequent lobbyists of big business. It has a broad depth of diverse and highly intelligent individuals who contribute to all aspects of social cohesion community and employee productivity. As Katie and I do not represent any of the above (50/50 Rule) so also do millions of other decent people. I see my (50/50 Rule) as a sad reflection of various academic or political theories over the years. "We are indeed the lucky country. It is a pity it is full of second-class citizens" – as White commented many years ago. When my rule was approximately 20/20. It has a causal link and requires radical surgery so to speak.

Government policy has undisputedly failed. When, by way of dramatic portrayal, a grossly overweight individual waddles into the medical centre with a magnitude of ailments, serious and minor, supported by a myriad of overlapping prescriptions. When that person drinks three cases of beer or spirits mixers per week, two packets of cigarettes a day, spend four nights a week *gambling in the RSL, eating chips and nuts. Eats regularly at Subway, McDonald's, KFC, Dominos and dozens of other similar products inclusive of large quantities of Coke, Pepsi sundae or a thick shake. All perfectly acceptable when eaten in moderation whilst supported with fruit, vegetables, legumes, pasta and so forth. They then may suggest that they struggle to survive on a pension. So, would any individual if they lived like this. 50% of Australia's population have failed, the education system has failed and consequently, the government has failed. We should have rights to freedom of choice – not so however if that lifestyle impacts upon the future wellbeing of others, the community and the country.*

Our lives progressed. Many holidays both within Australia and overseas. As my father often said, "Travel and the understanding of different cultures and lifestyles is the greatest education a person can have." The irony is that the old man had never been out of the UK; nonetheless, I now believe he was correct.

Katie's health was not detrimental to her career (I can only remember three sick days in around 40 something years). Whilst we scheduled her respective hospital procedures as a no-pay period, I would add that her employer always paid her the applicable salary. I doubt this would occur in the greed-driven shareholder return objectives of today. It was greatly appreciated and proved 'you only truly get back what you put in', as with anything in life. Loyalty and result were still appreciated, not as today as algorithms dominate.

Finally, in 1986 Katie received 'open-heart surgery'. It was a traumatic time for her, as she truly believed she would not survive. We had engaged in an extremely healthy regime of activity and lifestyle. We didn't smoke, very limited alcohol (well Katie anyway), salads, fruit, vegetables lean fresh meat, fish, cereals, legumes and definitely no takeaway. We did not drink carbonated soft drinks, only water, had limited our coffee intake to one cup per day, black no sugar. She was prepared. The operation was a 100% success and we moved from intensive care to a private ward and home very quickly. The other man, the (50/50 Rule) regrettably did not survive! Same brilliant surgeon, same conditions – please give this some thought. We are masters of our own destiny irrespective of gene theory.

She was back at work within 5-6 weeks, full bore. Maggie Thatcher, her character image, was back in charge. Dr Paul Russell, a brilliant and well-regarded cardiologist (still today 2019) has guided her heart issues and as a consequence, we have been immensely grateful. That, as medical innovation immerged applicable to her condition, we received it.

The years crept by and a healthy active lifestyle prevailed and, other than a well-managed heart, regime: with minimal medication, we came closer to the later part of our careers.

Katie's company had been restructured and underwent a buyout by a new holding group. This was a team of highly enthusiastic and motivated individuals and the usual 'younger thinking, positive work ethic'. I am not suggesting that Katie had in any way reduced her effort or result. More so, through experience, to work smarter. However, this renewed enthusiasm and opportunity invigorated her and she unrealistically recreated a work schedule applicable to a 'switched on' 30-year-old, not someone closer to 60. She loved the new initiatives and, as had always occurred, was given more responsibility, including export. This all went well for a few years.

As we both had our respective careers, we had always supported one another in our pursuits, and, as I have always succeeded all persons with ability and aptitude irrespective of gender or ethnicity etc., who was I to question my own wife. I nearly regretted that discussion. This is one time that I should have intervened as, over a period of time, she started to show signs of uncharacteristic lethargy, sleeping later on weekends, out of breath after more strenuous hill climbs, etc.

I received a phone call late afternoon to say she had been involved in a car accident and that she was all right, would organise the necessary logistics and call a taxi to bring her home. What appeared to have happened is that her vehicle had 'sideswiped' another car. Fortunately, both parties were not injured and the cars could be repaired. I believe she had encountered a nano nap and bang. I now realise that this instance was quite possibly the commencement of Dementia identifiers. Not then understood or considered.

We organised a specialist appointment, an echocardiogram and then an angiogram. The mitral valve appeared to have reduced to 1.2, a dangerous level of operation and she was subsequently booked into hospital for the next two days.

I make a note at this point that this process all occurred with no waiting. No bureaucracy, no contradiction as to medical problems. A new procedure was being trialled by Professor Ross recommended by Dr Russell. This opportunity was a result of the private, not public system. A system whose waiting lists are now far longer than then. A neighbour recently had heart problems. Within the public system, it took some months just to determine both the problem and subsequent angiogram and then the relative wait for the elective operation. Putting further strain on both physical and mental health.

Katie's operational procedure was a total success. Exceptional expertise and medical innovation had triumphed; however, I suggested that we should contemplate retirement. Now 60 years of age she had paid her dues. It was now our time to enjoy our hard-earned retirement, consequently, two months later we found ourselves at home – 24/7.

We quickly discovered that we both needed more than just a hobby, travel, reading etc. We had been boaties for many years having owned a number of models, starting our interest in the early '70s.

I suggested a 'project'. Reluctantly, as usual, Katie agreed, we commenced the process of finding a quality hull that required T.L.C. What we eventually found was an exceptionally well-regarded model, A Savage Sports fisher, commonly referred to as a "pocket" rocket. We had owned a similar model in the early eighties. Twin small block V8 318 Chryslers, double forward, starboard dining to double fold down and bathroom to port. She had sat on a mooring for many years, always with well-meant intentions, nonetheless now a very sad reflection of once former pride. We gutted her completely, rebuilt everything that required rebuilding. New instruments, motors, wiring, etc, and what resulted was brilliant. This project was completed in 2013.

So, what do we do next? What you always do, pack some suitcases, load the 4WD and head for the bush. One month to three months, no schedule.

As we headed around the country, we stayed in a number of caravan parks, something we had not previously done, as we had always preferred bush camping remote locations. Definitely in my case a throwback to the many times camping with my Aunt and Uncle or working on the farm and then the 'Flinders Ranges exposure'. As we travelled, the topic of investment and lifestyle emerged, specific to the purchase of a motel or caravan park. I started to look into the financial aspects of both, employment to operation, R.O.I's, trending, demographics etc, and it showed that at this point in time, the caravan park option offered better cash flow, whilst at the same time a less restricted workload and lifestyle, than motels. Specifically, for our available budget, the answer was a unanimous, No, No and No. If you think I am cleaning toilets, making beds, washing floors you will be doing it on your own. Patience Phil, this one might take some time and justification, develop a five-year business model, specifically how much money the skinflint can save. Well, that theory did not work. No and no. Maybe she is coming around, only two nos.

I certainly needed something to do in life. I am of the firm belief that people die young because of boredom, lack of real simulation or just sitting around on a humungous herd ship, stuffing themselves as a consumptive tourist, visiting ports for four hours, rummaging around like idiots and believing, that they now understand the peoples of that particular port or country from such a short-term disembarkation. A wonderful critical mass business model, if you own it, as opposed to the hundreds of people we have met, that create an extremely healthy and active lifestyle, volunteering in community activities, engaging in stimulating options and often engaging in part-time work endeavours. These people are the opposite of my (50/50 Rule). They give, not just expect or take. Fortunately, Australia still has millions of these individuals.

I kept 'working on Katie'. "That it would be tremendous to work together." She was not so sure that was actually a good idea. "We could purchase a business somewhat run down in the right location, add value and management."

"You are always buying run down things and doing them up properties, boats –No."

"We would ensure both lifestyle and income stream." Income stream, she kept warming – still no. Then it hit me. "You will be in charge totally; I will do the financial/cash flow and lawns. You can tell me what to do." Pause, silence.

"I will agree, however, stipulate that I will never do any of the physical activity. Simply customer service and reception, administration and staff rostering."

"Agreed." Consequently, that was the start of the next chapter of my career. As a lawn mowing contractor, reporting to an ageing Maggie Thatcher theorist.

We contacted various brokers throughout Australia, embarking on both a holiday and caravan park discovery, travelling some 14,000 km in the process. We looked at good ones, terrible ones, opportunists. Indeed, one in a particular location the sellers upped the price from $975,000 to $1.5 million with the discovery that we were from Sydney. Another told us that they had to sell the property urgently (the husband had aggressive terminal cancer). They were asking $1.1 million. I did my own searches and discovered that they had bought the property six months earlier for $395,000, tarting it up so to speak. Relisting it back onto the market, expecting both a mug and a quick buck. They were (both) there four years later? Buyer beware one could say, or maybe they were in my (50/50 Rule).

1. My Mother 1950

2. My Mother, Father – Little Lord Fauntleroy – Whitby

3. Charles – Hairdressing Salon Northallerton

4. Louise and I – Adelaide 1971

5. Katie and I – Dinner for Colonel and Mrs Sanders

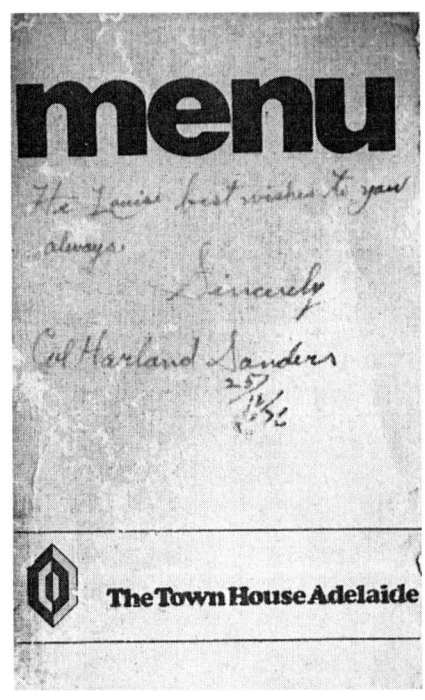

6. Menu signed for Louise

7. Katie and I – Phuket Early 80's

8. Me 1984

9. Katie – 1989

10. Two Tough Ladies – Berowra Waters 2013

11. Reunification Station (D. M. Z.) South Korea 2016

4) A Caravan Park, Alcoholic's Amyloids, Carcinoids and Charity

We finally settled on a run-down business in Mount Gambier, South Australia, the second-largest city in the state. We developed our business plans, locked up our home in Sydney (leaving Jerry, our very competent gardener, pool cleaner to look after the place) and started to reform a two-star wreck into a three-and-a-half-star destination option for mid socio(trades)demographics, targeting specific suburbs in both Adelaide and Melbourne with secondary country markets in South Australia and Victoria.

In the heart of the city, it had been a magnet for drunks, dole cheats, drug dealers and itinerate workers. Consequently, the local community, police and council welcomed our vision for revitalisation.

This became our first exposure to the marginalised, small think bureaucracy and charity misuse and misrepresentation.

We employed specific individuals, contracted to undertake the allocated work we had budgeted for. We sought and very quickly received support from the council and our plans for redevelopment were subsequently approved. This then saw the first instance of autocracy.

We discovered that a building structure on the title, developed into a laundromat many years before, was indeed the first building constructed in the locality circa1850 and it had significant history, murders and indeed the first hanging in the colonies. Also, various other uses: bank, grocery store, school, boarding house. We employed a local historical to research in totality inclusive of developing photographic date timelines. Our plan submitted to the council was to redevelop the rear of the laundromat into backpacker accommodation and lounge/kitchenette. The floors had all collapsed, the ceilings in two rooms were rotten, and the whole place had dry rot, salt damp and broken windows. The council, delighted and extremely supportive of our findings and objectives, approved our plans. Then disaster struck. Local heritage in Adelaide heard and as usual, bureaucracy saw an opportunity to 'make a name for themselves and spend someone else's hard-earned money'. It reminded me of many years before when I was asked to try and save a business entity and possibly the marriage of a young couple. Both teachers, who believed that it would be 'easy' to serve focaccia, tea, scones and coffee. They fell in love, as you do, with the concept of operating a café and the extremely inexpensive public authority lease terms. The request for my mediation had been through State and Regional development and I very quickly turned a disaster into a 'gold mine'. To the attention of the minister and it became an opportunity to sell the parties support of the small business. TV and interviews followed, much talk, congratulations, as to what the department had achieved. However, only one thing that was forgotten in the dialogue. It was Phil McLean and his associates in marketing and design that enhanced the status, not a politician. Another lesson in life.

The 'heritage man' dictated all types of requests, with no appreciation of business realities as to cost, viability and subsequent return. In particular, that whilst this building may be the first in the Mount, it was a poorly constructed, rough stone and fill structure on the interior with stone/brick exterior and no damp course. After much dictatorial frustration, I said, "put all of your requests, design plans, structural alterations on an official request and I will pay for the cost for your recommendations." Bureaucracy and indecision never make a real commitment in life and having called his bluff, I was left alone. I never got nor paid for any such information. We renovated as to normal and traditional building specifications, of historical significance. Replaced floors with original 1850 Baltic pine, purchased from an old warehouse in Adelaide and completed the project to an appropriate cost. The council approved its completion. We renovated the laundrette, told the history in narrative and pictures on the walls of the era and re-named the business 'The Banque', conscious of the original usage as a bank and general store in 1852. The 'little man' called in and was immensely impressed with the limewash walls that he had instructed. I didn't tell him it was actually Dulux suede effects which look somewhat like limewash nor did he ever ask to see original plans which depicted the original building, twice the size, nor look into the attic area. The original 1850-shingle roof was still in place, overbuilt with a second corrugated iron roof in the early 1910s. A typical authoritative manner if one challenges, with no real skills. Just abused the use of power and the legislation that protects. Why allow a listed building to fall into such disrepair over many years and respective owners, only to subject a well-intentioned individual the significant cost of the rebuild, whilst others had subsequently allowed that disrepair to magnify, spending nothing, when, on listing the property years before, the authority could have stipulated a caveat that ensured ongoing and annual financial upgrades, maintaining the integrity of the building for future generations. The market would have subsequently determined value, serviceability and return on investment, not a public servant.

The Banqué launderette became a successful part of the overall business entity, well patronised by locals and tourists alike.

Our health was fine. Katie showed no negative signs of health-related issues and I as normal was as fit as a Mallee Bull. I had been extremely lucky with my health since the car accident in my teens or maybe it's my genes. Other than the cardiac risk in my twenties, (16-hour days were not a good idea for one's health) I had experienced nothing of any significance. The odd bout of upset stomach and that was about it. As usual a stupid indestructible male. Katie had regular heart check-ups and all specialists were extremely pleased with their respective 'handy work'.

The park continued its development. I forgot to mention, within weeks of purchase we moved all the undesirables out. We had sought both legal and police advice on this matter prior to purchase terms. We implemented the plan. That, whilst unleased by the previous owners, the tenants could have called on their rights, given some had experienced lengthy periods of stay. We, fortunately, had no repercussions. Not so many new owners in other locations, who experienced great difficulty with eviction notices. We discovered a drug laboratory that had clearly been in situ for some years. An interesting female aided by 'the system' living in a 25-foot caravan, she actually owed six weeks rent, had five children under eight years of age to five different partners. Shake it up Phil, this is the real world. No longer a one-off mistake, our bureaucracy now actually paid people to have babies. One couple had secured welfare, rent support, two children already (not his) and a baby. The baby bonus cheque arrived and he bought a Holden Ute. They moved out and three weeks later, he was 'cruising' the main street with another young lost soul. Five hundred and sixty thousand single mothers in Australia at the time. (50/50 Rule).

I told three elderly men that they were welcome to stay, that we would be renovating their rented caravans, certifying gas (not done for years), supplying fire alarms, extinguishers and connecting to underground coaxial cable for TV.

Old Max and Henry were retired shearers, the real salt of the earth Aussie. Drank little, smoked like chimneys and were well received by tourists in their experiences of life's banter. However, Bruce was an alcoholic. A man, who received his pension, paid his rent, bought his food supplies and paid his electricity in advance. He then sat in his caravan for four days, drank himself stupid, then 'sort of sobered up' till he received money to repeat the exercise over when the next payment arrived from Centrelink, and here I am thinking that I had seen it all. Wrong again – back on a learning regime.

We had employed a cleaning team from day one, which had grown to three. I was the gardener and lawn contractor, dog's body in all. "Yes darling, anything you say, darling." We had a management team alternatively working three weeks in the park, and in our case, three weeks travelling back to our home in Sydney or going away for a short holiday. It was a great lifestyle.

Next comes my first encounter with both charities and human services. I would add that they are just 'the public service', not the Government. Certainly not an appropriate care opportunity. The staff we encountered bogged down in more and more indecision, totally incapable of reacting to individual needs. Unable, in the hierarchal environment, to make impromptu decisions, even if they had the skill or desire to do so.

Bruce had lost his family, friends and all pride in his own capacity. I tried giving him work, which he did well with dignity. Unfortunately, as soon as I paid him, his cycle of self-abuse immediately re-commenced, breaking the traditional fortnightly routine of drinking for a given period, then time-limited sobriety.

When he was drunk, he retired to his caravan and would not come out, except for toiletry, which he would schedule until after dark when the park amenities were quiet. He did however use the bucket and then emptied it into the toilet. I decided that we had to do something.

His family listened to me about that which they already knew. "Thanks, but no thanks. We have done this for years; we are not doing it again." So, I started what became a two-week frustrating waste of time of trying to access the dozens of services that cater for Bruce's, and persons like him, specific needs. In short, it was all too damn hard for these taxpayer-funded care institutions or charities, which actually did not give a damn.

There were privacy matters. "For god sake woman he is dying, he needs help, sorry Mr McLean you could try 'x y' and 'z'." All a waste of time, no one including a council friend had the will or guts to commit to his support needs.

It was a Friday afternoon and I decided, as I have not seen him for some time that I would check his caravan. What I found was an unbelievable mess. I went to Lifeline, now 5:30 pm and closed. The response to my request I will never forget to this day. Pressing the intercom. "Hi it's Phil McLean from Central Caravan Park, I have a resident, an alcoholic, Bruce, and I'm am concerned for his health and wellbeing, could you give me some advice or support?"

Reply, "Call an ambulance."

"Is that it?"

"You can come back on Monday."

I cannot repeat what my response was. A doctor said that I should remove the alcohol and his inebriation would wear off. Clearly, old Bruce was well known, even if this church abiding caring community and public welfare structure did not give a damn. No doubt, they would go to his funeral and the eulogy would read quotations as to what a wonderful man he had been.

I revisited the Salvation Army and received the same response. So, I wrote to the Major (or some such title) in Adelaide head office. Demanding that this godly institution get off their backside and revisit their original charter, he not only responded, but he also organised detox for Bruce in Portland Victoria.

I waited until Bruce was responsive and discussed the option with him. He was concerned as to being on his own. So, in reviewing the situation with Max and Henry, we advised him that we would take him to Portland and visit him regularly. He agreed. I have always, rightly or wrongly communicated what I expected and advised Bruce that he must realise, that, whilst we would do everything in our power to support him, he must help himself. As such, if he would not help, I would not accordingly allow him to reside in this park. He actually thanked me for being straightforward and honest with him. A few days later, the four of us drove to Portland. The positive objective is to supporting Bruce, booking into detox, comfortable and on his first walk to better health and wellbeing.

The Major broke down all the bureaucratic bulldust and we were given privy to access and discuss his particular circumstances, what we knew of his background, family and medical condition.

This is briefly, what happened. After induction, medical examination and physiological assessment etc., Bruce, extremely happy and excited, informed me, "Everything is fine Phil; they told me that I need not worry, I'm in good shape and need not come into detox."

This is again briefly that which the specialist told me: "Bruce has an extremely long non-violent history of alcoholism. His medical condition has and continues to deteriorate as a result of alcoholic consumption. His liver has chronic complications and his mental capacity is significantly reduced and damaged as a result of the long-term alcoholism. However, Phil, whilst he needs care desperately, sadly we cannot make the person commit if they will not accept the problem. I am dreadfully sorry; we see this situation regrettably all too often."

Bruce left the park shortly after this episode, ultimately leaving for Queensland with Gary. Actually, when the government of the day, coming to an election, announced a one-off welfare payment to all disability pension recipients of $500, inclusive of petrol monies to relocate if they so desired. I was told that he had spent a few nights sleeping rough near the railway tracks and that none of the welfare groups had visited. The lucky country.

Katie and I both started to show specific health issues. Hers, loss of memory and un-characteristically making mistakes with Excel, Word and specifically, the time to perform relatively simple administrative procedures.

Mine to hot flushes and body heat, stomach bloating and cramps.

In Katie's situation, a few visits back to Sydney specialists and it was decided that the hernia pronounced by a GP was indeed the left hip. Arthritic and in need of replacement urgently. No specialist would commit as to who was the best surgeon for this procedure.

Johnson and Johnson were in court both, in the States and Australia, as to failed prostheses, types of material composition etc., and the resultant patient outcome. So, in my usual always go to the top mantra, who would the Queen go to, or a Packer, Lowy? My searches resulted in the Mater, North Sydney and the specialist, Michael Sullivan. Katie said, "As he sounded Irish, he must be good." He did some three hundred operations per year and his team, extremely well practised only performed hip operations. Golden staphylococcus was some 500 in each 10,000. Whereas in a similar public facility was 2000 per 10,000.

The decision was made and she was duly booked in for the operation and rehabilitation a few weeks later. Note private patient, weeks, public being elective months and months. Note: specialist and team, only hips. Not so the public system: hips, knees, hand and anything else that appears similar.

Michael convinced Katie that she need not concern herself regards a particular thought, she also once more believed that she was about to die. 'Mrs McLean, I perform some 300 operations per year and I have never experienced one leg being shorter than the other as a result of the procedure', and no one has ever died. I thought: well he is definitely not Irish. That's a joke, people.

My health problems became of some concern. I went to various GP's who requested numerous tests, always the same, some excuse. However, they could find nothing wrong with me.

Basically, I was an extremely fit 64-year-old. I was referred to a gastroenterologist who did more and more tests, yet another endoscopy and colonoscopy. Nothing, I had felt that various GP actually saw me as a hypochondriac (definitely not me) and finally sought an opinion from one more doctor. Katie came with me and after looking at my past result documentation he suggested that both we possibly needed a holiday. More concerned about Katie than I. "Well, you are 68 Mrs McLean, its hard work operating a caravan park."

"No, it's not; we have a team of colleagues to help. We are only on-site for three weeks each six."

"Well, I still think you need a holiday."

Two weeks later, we were in the Westin at Denarau, Fiji. Me feeling awfully sick and Katie getting lost within the resort complex. The holiday was a disaster and on return, my condition now the focus, I went to the Medical Centre and asked to see a young Chinese/Australian trained doctor, who had been highly recommended.

I spent my career surrounding myself with people with better skills and education than mine. Honours or better still a PhD let them run with it and give them full acknowledgement. I got the options recommended, made the decision, generally steering the ship in the right direction.

The first question after reviewing my tests is, "Do you think I am imagining this doctor? It cannot be serious otherwise I would be dead."

"No, I do not think it is psychological, it does not appear in character and we do have to determine what is causing your symptoms to ensure that it is not serious." So, it's off to the gastro again with a new set of thoughts.

He is on holiday however, the young locum can see you if you agree. Yes, of course. In I go. He had clearly paid great attention to my now rather extensive file of activity. He asked me a number of questions and advised me that he thought that I had a very rare form of tumour (no mention of cancer) and that he would like me to do some specific tests with urine, excrement and blood. The tests were conducted and more were requested. I was then called back to see the original gastroenterologist, now returned from the holidays.

He spluttered and coughed, looking at the report, not me, and advised that it was an extremely rare cancer (around 100 known in Australia). That it was inoperable. Right, so what happened to all the previous theories? "Red herrings Philip, just red herrings."

"Very good, I'm going to Italy in seven months, will that be okay?" (Always a different way to get the answer you actually want. Try and second-guess me).

"Yes, I think so, however, if things move quickly, we can organise a letter to get your travel monies returned."

"Right, that's good, a letter. So, is this terminal Doctor?"

"It's not good Philip."

"Right, so how long do I have?"

"It's not good Philip."

"How long?"

"Difficult to say, 12-14 months?"

Holy hell, I'm bloody dying and definitely not ready. What about Katie?

Only those who have been told will understand, these are a few of the words you do not wish to hear. I asked him what would happen next and he advised me that he would organise a consultation with a Professor Oncologist at Macquarie University Hospital. I actually didn't hear anything, I walked out in a daze and suggested to Katie we go for a coffee. I started to remember the charred bodies, consequently, in seconds it came back and I was determined to apply my 16-year-old psychology, there is always somebody worse off than you.

I told her that they had to do some more tests and that everything would be fine. The next lesson in life, never lie to a wife that you have never lied to. She knew instinctively and believe me; she knew me better than I. Whilst there were a few tears, my attitude was, "well where to, from here?" Do we start making plans, solicitors and the like?

I went into Gurney's office, Professor Howard Gurney to be precise, in my opinion now the best oncologist in this country. I was thinking India, ULCA or similar. He had obviously read my file, we discussed my condition, an extremely positive man and it was up and on. A particular medication is administered by injection and 'you will live for years'. A drug that suppressed the "tumours", slowing down the growth. Realistically eight years with what we know, however, with slow cancers like this specific type, it can depend on attitude and the individual. We subsequently discovered from Howard that 1% of all GPs would determine and diagnose in their total career, one person with this rarity. Am I lucky? Extremely, (a) because it progresses slowly, as long as it does not get to the pancreas and (b) it had only just been identified that a particular drug slowed the growth progression of the numerous tumours.

This brought us back to, 'take every day as an opportunity and get on with life'.

About this period Henry, who used to do the park rubbish collection and recycling for me, which gave him a good supplement to his pension, he identified with the "grey nomads", discussing his bush travels and his life was contented. He did however have a problem; he smoked, a great deal.

His health deteriorated relatively quickly, constantly displaying 'the smoker's cough'. If anyone has been associated with a person who has ultimately died, it's a particular guttural rattly sound. Instinctively you know, that it is not a positive sign of health. That life is indeed limited, here today, forgotten tomorrow.

I stopped listening to Henry objecting to a doctor visit, telling him that he was going to the hospital and that I was taking him, and that was it. He was admitted immediately and he never left, dying some five weeks later. He never wanted to know what was wrong with him, one of his final discussions with me stating, "Well, I am 63." Hell, I thought 83 was young. He was a nice man.

This was the time that I had my second awakening, charities. In so much the significant numbers registered and economic opportunists that they had become. Stretching funding allocation and the good faith of the public generosity.

When we purchased the park there was a shortlist of statements as to what not to do. The top two statements were:

- Never take charity collectors, they are thieving ratbags.
- Never book welfare paid individuals. They know how to work the system, possibly on drugs and will leave the cabin like a tip.

As the park had been extremely run down, in sales decline and, in our short tenure, we had paid little attention to the comments.

It is well known in caravan parks that if an owner has been 'tough' on the residents they will move on to elsewhere, specifically those with drug or alcohol problems. Completely out of the employment systems, whilst fully integrated into the welfare regime, they know how to work the system for all it is worth. Completely inexperienced and on a steep learning curve we were starting to understand with the help and support of the local police. I just make mention, policemen and women, paramedics alike deserve medals for what they have to endure. Those that we came to know were brilliant in supporting our endeavours. I could write a book on caravan park life on its own.

Back to charities. Those organisations which had been banned previously started to request accommodation bookings. Generally, for one week, miss a week, and then back again. They were certainly well behaved, leaving cabins clean and tidy. So why would you ban them? Its income. The initial bookings were made by head office. The protocol was to take a deposit (no deposit, no booking) with the remainder of the monies paid on arrival. The deposit was paid and we were advised, "The team leader was management and has the authority to pay and would do so on arrival." They arrived, just an ordinary group of young sociable backpackers. No money. They phoned head office and after some heated discussion, the funds were deposited. They advised, that they were collecting for something like Cystic Fibrosis, they left after a week, absolutely no trouble or behavioural problems.

Two weeks later same issue, no money and in this instance the head office would not pay. They told us that they would be back shortly with the money. Half the $400 plus accommodation cost in $2.00 coins, the rest in crumpled notes. This week they would be collecting for the Sturt Football Club, next time the Heart Foundation.

Over the next few months, more organisations booked and similar situations occurred. One group operated its head office in Point Piper, the wealth belt in Sydney's Eastern suburbs. One-week maybe a football club another heart, dementia, or diabetes organisation. The whole gambit of charity immerged. Clearly, Mount Gambier 'was a good demographic for suckers'.

We started getting buskers, obviously good returns; they paid in $100 bills, admitting to earning $400/$500 on a good day. Then the individual collectors, for a particular charity, or their own charity. Always the same story, someone had died, or very ill. A close friend, son, daughter, wife. I started to think this may be an abuse of regular charities or possibly deceit and as such that the generous public was being deceived. Maybe this fits into my (50/50 Rule). 50% ripping off the system, 50% genuine. We discovered that the companies paid commission and that the collectors received 40% of that collection. The question is, who determined what was collected? This was definitely not your grandmother's lamington drive. The individuals, bikers, runners, walkers, billy carts, you name it we saw it. Particularly the overseas or interstate persons, they certainly had a good holiday. The final straw came when two things occurred:

- I remember something that my father said when I was ten or eleven years old.
- We found dozens of opened collection "cans" in the rubbish solos after we had been paid accommodation costs with $500 in gold coins.

Firstly, my father's lesson in life. My father, an extremely generous man, had supported all manner of racial integration after the war, a Mason and its charitable offering plus his helping individuals periodically. I remember a great many Jewish friends, Polish and Hungarian who had suffered in the 40s. He had immense respect for the Polish airmen enlisted into the RAF or whatever reason he always spoke highly of Indians and Ghurkha. The northeast at this point was suffering an economic decline in its steel industry production and the population was predominately hard-working class people. Living in a traditional two up two down terraces house (the style seen in the TV program Coronation Street). The general mode of transport in the '50s was a bicycle in these specific demographics.

My father's car at the time was a Mark 10 Jaguar. We drove past a particular house outside of which stood a Jaguar. "Do you see the car son?"

"Yes, Dad," That man, he named him, is a union rep. (electrician) and he has started a charity collecting money for Ethiopian children. Now, how is it that this man can afford a Jaguar on an electrician salary? Rightly or wrongly and certainly not degrading a trade. Persons could not get loans, credit cards or car finance as most people could do today. I will never give money to a charity again and he never did. However, on numerous occasions I watched him give money to 'down on their luck' individuals. He may have been right, or wrong, the man may have received the money in a will or by other perfectly legal means. I leave you to judge. I think in hindsight my father was right. Years later, I saw where that man lived, still an electrician and union rep. He no longer lived in a terrace but a superb palatial home! Maybe both me and my father were wrong! Given that which we encountered has led me to believe that ultimately the process of charitable and non-government not for profit organisations will be challenged.

This past thought from 50 years ago plus the park circumstances annoyed me and I subsequently wrote to a female minister, Jane Lomax-Smith, in the South

Australian government. Detailing succinctly, I detailed the facts as had occurred, inclusive of companies (charities), not for profit organisations, individuals and names/addresses. I never received a reply, all too hard, just like the recent banking commission.

I am of the firm belief that the taxpayer-funded social welfare programs, not for profits, charities require a comprehensive review. That indeed there is in this country an oversupply of duplicated provider services whereby funding may well not be going to the intended objective. Hierarchal bureaucracy in both public service and charitable organisations may well be 'soaking up' much-needed funding from the 'coalface' and that in the specific case of the oversupplied charitable domain the varying degrees of monies collected, unrealistic to the intended reason. Specifically, those issues are experienced periodically where there was potential fraud, theft, misrepresentation of purpose 'creating a nice lifestyle' for many persons, paid for by the generosity of generous well-meaning Australians.

Katie and I enjoyed our lifestyle of three weeks on, three weeks off, consolidating our semi-retirement, visiting both friends and relatives overseas. However, whilst my health was being supported by leading-edge medication and specialists, Katie's memory issues continued to raise concern. Her hip operation had been 100% successful, her heart was well managed all this left was the head.

I would have work tasks to do outside, take guests to cabins, caravan groups onto their sites etc. and on return I would find her not completed basic email response to enquiries, phone calls had been forgotten or a cash flow statement would exhibit a profit or loss of $10,000.00, while it may be $100.00 as such incorrect data being produced. All totally and completely out of character. Her respective references had all been glowing as to her administrative credit and customer serviceability. I had never experienced this until our "joint capacity of employment" and it became apparent that we had greater problems than thought. She had installed all the systems and procedures that we had developed and agreed upon with simple efficiency. Training staff and management with great ease and enjoyment, now not remembering those procedures.

While you have GPs suggesting that these memory lapses are normal age-related decline in memory, you tend to listen initially, in my case, not for very long. After almost 50 years in an intimate relationship, one becomes one. You almost know what the other is thinking. Our joke being Katie is the boss, what's mine is Katie's and what's Katie's is hers.

I requested a referral to a geriatrician, much to the annoyance and denial of my dear wife.

Those experienced with the knowledge or thought of adaptation to those with dementia will note, that in many instances this is an extremely difficult time to navigate. Whilst a son, daughter, sister or brother is telling you (or by action think) that 'mum, dad, gran or grandpa is just getting older', they, you or the person with the illness is in denial. Extremely common within the Australian demeanour.

The longer all parties continue this denial, the more they miss and, most importantly, the time that they have remaining to enjoy the opportunities that they may have planned, travel, garden, hobbies, reading, painting. This will all be diminished, indeed, when a person is diagnosed with a specific form of dementia, you should suggest the difficult activity is attempted first. To the extreme, if you plan a cycling holiday around Italy, a hike to the base camp at Everest, a caravan trip for nine months around Australia or Canada, do it first, it will in time be impossible and you will regret having not tried.

Dementia manifests in many guises and each individual has different reactions affecting lifestyle. The earlier a person receives (a) specific diagnosis and (b) support structures, the less difficult the journey will be as the illness progresses.

A specialist informed me there are two types of person, nasty and nice. The first will continually fight the actions of the illness which of course causes disruptive moments, and nice, those that fight the disease and not a carer.

Yes, you guessed it, I got nasty. God bless her. Mrs Thatcher eat your heart out. And me such a quiet agreeable chap. What a great combo.

That is not for one moment to suggest that you as the carer or the person with the illness should not fight the disease – just not each other.

Dr Jerome IP, Geriatrician referred Katie for studies (640 participants) to the Ageing Mind and Brain Centre Camperdown, Sydney, NSW. They further diagnosed Alzheimer's supported by various CT/PET scans and we started the journey.

Initially, the symptoms, which apparently differ from person to person, were confusing with clinical tasks. A change in writing pattern, computing skills and Katie would not just loose the car keys; she would not remember where the car was parked. Simple housekeeping procedures would either take longer or create difficulty – simple routines like putting a pillowcase over the pillow, putting a tea bag into the sugar bowl rather than the cup and pouring water into the sugar or an empty cup.

I remember on her last trip to Australia in her mid-70s, Katie's mother was having problems and we just put it down to 'getting older'. Even when getting lost in Changi airport (Singapore) on her way home, eventually being found outside the airport terminal, she was undeterred as others rushed to organise an alternative flight. Lack of personal care or worry often develops with changes in mood or similarly others can become extremely confused.

On a trip to South Korea in 2016, while changing planes at Changi, I lost Katie (déjà vu). iPhones and facial recognition are wonderful tools, we found her within 10 minutes, in tears and distraught. I had taken her to a female toilet, which was advised as having only had one way in with the same way out, I stood and waited. Nothing, there was actually another way out. Not remembering "markers", Katie had come out of the other door. From that point in time, I have always taken her to disability toilets. Lesson learnt.

Whilst her symptoms worsened, she showed no outward signs of any illness. As with my Carcinoid, I just looked like any 60 something healthy individual. As with doctors, in not finding a prognosis, unspoken words from family or friends suggesting a belief that an exaggeration of facts or health severity is occurring, which of course means no support is given. There is also the ageing discussion of relative health issues. As such, that their arthritic hand or aching back, has the same implications as Cancer or Alzheimer's. "You both look so fit and well, how was your trip to Mexico and Cuba?" It's almost a pre-determined question – well if you can do that trip you can't be too unhealthy.

There is also the lack of traditional outward signs of illness, limping, wheezing, loss of weight and gaunt features etc. which you do not display, so it, therefore, can't be serious. To this day with Katie, who has always had what could best be described as a young phone voice, and people who have spent no time with her (including our daughter), will take a long time to grasp the severity and cruel outcome of this illness, by which time it is too late, it is all lost and one can never go back.

I remember a very dear older friend, Fred Hocking, devastated that he had not seen his mother in the last week when she had died suddenly on a Friday. For years, irrespective of outings, he would call in early each Thursday to see how she was. It highlights the need to live in the present because in many instances the past is lost extremely quickly.

We took the decision to sell the business and the process was a relatively straightforward action.

We spent time with the new owner until acquainted with the various procedures and said goodbye to many new friends and acquaintances.

Whilst we had no real option but to sell, given the health prognosis, I would suggest that 'work is not a dirty word'. I am of the firm belief that all the obvious benefits aside, an activity as long as practical takes one's mind off self-pity and most importantly boredom. You can only catch so many fish, play so many games of golf and have so many hobbies. Whilst I am not suggesting you should not do all of the above if you so desire, however, mental and some degree of disciplined work activity, definitely maintains wellbeing longer.

I would like to comment on my fore-mentioned (50/50 Rule). That inappropriate lifestyle choices are having a significant impact upon both our mental and physical health.

Both Katie and I have age longevity in our ancestry. Other than war-related causes, TB, smoking bombs, subsequently all our relatives lived into their 80s and 90s. My mother's brother died recently aged 97. As I have said earlier, I believe that the reason for Katie's Alzheimer's could be linked back to rheumatic fever in childhood and in my case outback uranium/mineral enriched bore water.

However, as a community, a considerable degree of our health outcomes can be attributed to our lifestyle choices – deliberate or demographic.

If your family or friends have an illness or are showing potential signs of one, I would implore you to try and convince them to alter their lifestyle. This country has possibly one of the best medical local networks in the world; we just need to go looking. It has to be our choice, however as an extremely "lucky country," it should also be our responsibility not to burden future generations with this cost impasse.

(50/50 Rule). Over the past 50 years and each successive decade, we have seen consistent growth in those previously mentioned population categories. I use the (50/50 Rule) to highlight the significance of the combined issues, appreciating that the data shows higher than 50% in all categories. Compared to 7-8% in the 1960s. This is not the profile of a forward-thinking, productive and cohesive population. I would suggest that they all have a causal link. This is definitely not a populist subject. However, we are certainly in denial. Men, in

many instances refusing to accept the impact that their actions are having on others.

QUOTE: Most men would rather die than change – most do.
Bernard Russell

We must take responsibility for our own actions and the old statement, "we are what we eat and drink," is indeed true. To compare our statistical negativity in the associated habits, to read the data over five decades, to ignore the signs and make weak imputation and representation is almost criminal. If a company allowed its employees to drink, gamble or take drugs in the course of employment what would happen? You all know what would happen. Why then, have successive Governments failed to support its people arriving at this position of (50/50 Rule). 1. Obesity, 2. Alcoholic overuse, 3. Gambling and drug addiction. 4. Overmedicated as a partial result of 1, 2 and 3. Not to forget the magnitude of domestic or social violence and breakdown in relationships. It is not that government do not have the appropriate options; they do. It's that the toughest decisions are not what people may like and therefore politicians take the easier path. I have always believed that I would rather (in deep regret and sadness) sacrifice six to save 60. Politicians sacrifice nothing and lose thousands. That said, I am a total believer in freedom of choice. You have the right to eat as much as you wish and in whatever format. Similarly, with alcohol and gambling. However, if that freedom creates mental and medical crises in your body, should you expect others to pay for your lack of control? Well, let me tell you this, western democracies will not be able to afford you in 50 years, consequently, you will have to resolve your own problems by then, regardless of your wants.

With "fatness" we can generally expect illness, some through genetics, some possible disease, others metabolism, even sex, yes, it's widely referred that some enjoy sex with overweight persons, they get their kicks by domineering fatter people.

This however is not the norm. The reality of the magnitude of these problems have occurred in the past 50 years and specifically, Western society. Consider photographic history, your 1960 school photographs, the sports field, the samplings, one fat individual in the class, now it's 60%. Visit any food court afternoon when schools are out and see what these children are eating and drinking.

No moderation here. Its 24/7 junk food advertising and addictive comfort food with no consideration to moderation, digestion or future health, mental as well as physical outcomes. Fatness is the new norm.

A quote: Stuffed and Starved – Markets, Power and the Hidden Battle for the World Food System. Raj Patel.

"The increased availability of food (especially sugary, snack food, or any other) targeted at children, together with an environment in which children are able to effectively howl for it, and in which this pester-power is leveraged by markets, has led to explosions in children's ill health."

Brand leaders such as Nestle or Kraft have manipulated addictive-based products, easily prepared and retailed clearly as a commodity.

-Enzymatic digestion/chemical hydrolysis

-Syrups and sugars

-Sodium/salts

Leaders in the 19th century such as Henri Nestle, James Kraft, Forrest Mars and George Cadbury – to mention a few, built brands on trust and quality. Fast forward to the 1950s and we see the commenced amalgamations and manipulation of the product. Now owned by multinational/investment hedge funds, their only objective being brand dominance/shareholder greed with no consideration to the consumer's health – both physical and mental. No different to the final outcome with tobacco. Both addictive. Both will kill you. The chain of events starts with the producers or manufacturer of the goods, branded and often low in nutritional goodness. Sold cheaply at retail.

Quote – Brogan – our new masters. 1947

The people have been deceived most certainly, but they wanted to be deceived, they have voted against the modest expectations of life, which are also what a sober public man can ever strive for. They have voted to eat their cake and have it to save it for a rainy day and to give it away. They have voted for high wages and low production and a world of plenty. They have voted like the courtiers of King Canute, who planted his seat before the encroaching waves and commanded them to retire by authority of the Royal and unimpeachable will. The people are able to fill the seat with the sovereignty of their own choosing. Nobody denies their right. But the tide keeps coming in.

5) Incompetence, Incontinence and a Royal Commission Showcase

With the park sold and re-established back in our Sydney home for longer periods, we realised very quickly that our idyllic retirement-built home on the banks of the Hawkesbury River was not now the appropriate location. Easily accessible, nonetheless quiet remote for specific services and daily needs. We contemplated the future, in specific terms, what indeed would occur if I were to die before Katie and how that would impact upon her from a survival standpoint, as Alzheimer's 'set in'.

Our boat was on a marina berth close by. We did have water access at home, however, the "rowing to and from the boat" was proving more difficult and potentially dangerous. The marina provided social aspects plus walk-on access. Cast off, tie up and walk off. Extremely civilised.

At this point in time my illness was accepted, however never to be defeated, managed. My special-order script costing thousands of dollars was a testament to the country's Medicare options, private health insurance, a medical breakthrough in cancer research and palliative care. The internal side effects were at times dreadful, nausea, hot flushes, incredible body heat, rashes and headaches. Never together, never knowing what it will be – the worse being nausea. Far worse than any car crash, indeed, like anything experienced before. I have a high tolerance for pain, whilst nausea at times leaving you to think is this worth it? Mimicking chemo and the resultant side effects. Thank heavens, as it gets, and will continue to become worse, I have only wanted to die twice. When it's over you get on with it. I sometimes think that the mind puts your own health issues into a separate component when managing someone to care for. You become more concerned for them than yourself.

My uncle Ray died recently aged 97, probably from a broken heart, five weeks after my aunt had suffered a massive heart attack and subsequently died.

The mind can be good; the mind can be bad depending on your own willpower and determination. Maybe it's also a 'we' not 'me' upbringing?

The gardens and pool started to take its toll on my physical capacity to undertake the tasks that I had always completed with ease and pleasure. Internally one becomes weary. It's a different type of tiredness. Whilst looking outwardly fit and healthy, the body as I now understand, slowly shutting down. Whilst my Carcinoid has metastasized to various organs, I thank my lucky stars it has not as yet touched the pancreas. If and when – good night Phil, very quickly.

We started looking for suitable 1st and 2nd option retirement localities. The boat (*marina berth*), the small unit easily cared for, nursing homes, hospital (private) doctors and good transport links. As part of Katie's heart medication (Warfarin), she feels the cold. Consequently, we started looking at options within Queensland, her choice, mine had been Bermagui for fishing and colder climate.

Our choices, after some six months of exploring both the north and the south seaboard, culminated in a choice of two suitable localities. Runaway Bay Queensland and Hawks Nest NSW. Hawks Nest as a community was favoured, however, it had neither a suitable marina nor fuel and the nearest acceptable hospital (the San/Norwest) was in Sydney. The nearest train (interstate) was Taree and it had a less temperate climate than Queensland for Katie.

Consequently, Runaway Bay was chosen. However, before this was to occur an operation was suggested regards Katie's dementia/Alzheimer's. Dr Jerome IP, a Geriatrician, suggested that Prof. Brian Owler had undertaken a number of procedures to remove fluid from the brain, generally used for the treatment of hydrocephalus.

Prof Owler met with us and agreed to perform this procedure. I had been researching the many and varied theories for Alzheimer's and was aware that a Professor at Copenhagen University was studying fluid extraction, toxins etc. To me, anything had to be better than sitting back watching your wife's health deteriorate. The operation involved the insertion of a valve into the brain cavity (Medtronic shunt) and tube to the stomach. The shunt removes a pre-set designated amount of fluid from the brain as build up occurs, therefore reducing pressure. Prof. Owler initially performed a spinal tap, advising that if any benefits were to be noticed, that one would see changed mood, memory and general behaviour within 24-48 hours. The results were profound – it was like going back six or seven years.

The operation was scheduled at The Sydney Adventist Hospital, Wahroonga. Having spent approximately 36 hrs in intensive care Katie was admitted to a hospital room, then five days of rehabilitation and we were home within 10 or 11 days. The difference was amazing. Prof Owler had advised initially that the procedure may have no effect in terms of memory/activity and indeed, if it did, it may only last for so long, eventually plateauing. The outcome was far more beneficial than we could have hoped for or expected. Only those living with a person in decline through dementia would appreciate the time that I believe this medical intervention gave us. I would suggest in the order of five years. In terms of slowing the progression of the associated symptoms and effects. Only the private system could have given us this opportunity, not to mention the specific skills of Prof. Owler. To him it was possibly another day at the office, to us, it will be something we will be forever grateful for.

We settled into Runaway Bay and both loved the area weather. A small easily managed unit overlooking the Broad Water Shores marina. Our boat never did see the marina; we moved it to Brooklyn marina adjacent to the Sydney-Brisbane freeway. I was still having my monthly Somatuline Lanreotide injection at Norwest, so we travelled (on holiday) to and from Sydney each month, using the boat as our unit on the water accommodation.

Katie's eldest sister and brother-in-law came over from Scotland for a visit and it was clear that Sadie had many problems. Unlike us, with National Scottish Health System the GP had diagnosed her. No scans, no PET, no in-depth physiological assessment (the Mind and Brain Centre takes approx. three hours) and no knowledge as to what type of dementia it possibly was.

I would suggest that any person noticing anything that is out of character seek medical assessment as quickly as possible and get a second opinion. Ensuring that you consult the appropriate specialist for diagnosis. Many ill-informed GPs have diagnosed dementia when it was actually a urinary tract infection – a situation easily resolved with a course of antibiotics.

Given Katie and Sadie's mother's health condition some years before, it is indeed advisable that siblings undertake the appropriate tests to determine if there is a possibility of a hereditary illness. Familial genetics of Alzheimer's.

Cancer, breast, many years ago was an unspoken topic. Thank goodness today, if grandmother had breast cancer, sensible individuals would have the appropriate tests to determine probability. Not so dementia. It is, for all the information content and support, still in many instances seen as taboo. Somebody passed a Freudian slip "lost her marbles" some weeks ago which relates to the 20 century – the workhouse and funny farm.

Friends, and indeed relatives, often both have difficulty dealing with the prognosis and the actually 'happenings'. Some communities are less prone to rejection, however; I give a recent example of how much we have changed in the acceptance.

We were in Scotland in late 2018, on route to four weeks in China, staying with Sadie and John at Dollar. It's the long way around however keeps the outlaws happy.

I was interested in comments written in numerous issues of The Tablet, the Catholic newsletter. The topic in question was male child abuse, both sexual and otherwise, the clergy and the years of denial and the church's attitude to homosexuality. Some comments were made by Australian journalists, the Wilson issues and the forthcoming Pell trial.

I asked John, "would the subject of homosexuality have been so openly discussed 5-10 years ago?" Phil – three things you never discussed, Death, Cancer and Homosexuality. Yet again, I must have grown up in a very open conversational environment, all topics agreed or otherwise, were on the table in the McLean household.

People look at you strangely, specifically if something occurs that 'in their small thinking mind' believe dreadful. For example, a supermarket. A raised voice – KATIE. As she wanders off, lost and the shoppers' looks will tell you, "What a horrible man, yelling at his wife like that." Katie has one earpiece and the hearing is confusing in noisy environments. It is difficult for her, unless you raise your pitch. You flash your green carer's card and quietly tell the usually fat ignoramus that your wife of 50 years has Alzheimer's. Why is it that fat people are always so bossy? Maybe Andy Capp was right, maybe it's Noddy and Big Ears, more probably a very poor education regime, single parent, and I am owed everything belief. (50/50 Rule).

You may have annoying moments whilst seated, drinking a coffee. Dementia sufferers will often portray signs of interest or affection to complete strangers. A casual smile and they will stop waiting for recognition or conversations. In the 'Nanny' overprotected environment that children have been raised in, parents, become concerned when 'that old lady' stops to talk to the children, the grandchildren she would have loved to have had possibly. The reaction is one of horror – a leper has been let loose in the shopping centre. I generally find that the lower the socio-economic demography, the worse the response. No longer the 'salt of the earth', the child is ripped away and this little old lady looks forlorn, hurt and lost.

Maybe the obvious (50/50 Rule), clearly on drugs or alcohol or both, Schizophrenia, works the system, wears long sleeves, good clothes and has a haircut for the regular court appearances for assault, drugs, criminality, you can now pick them easily. As a Sergeant of police said to me, "You know how your parents taught you, never judge a book by its cover," well you can. If they look like a social misfit, they generally are. So, beware if the dementia sufferer stares very unintentionally for too long. You will be abused if the particular individual is on that drug low point. In one instance, I was seriously threatened. An authoritative voice and quick explanation of Alzheimer's, and (as they are generally mentally weak) back down very quickly calling you 'sir'. Apologising for what had occurred, and in one instance, talking about the methadone they were taking. Clearly, at that instance, they had not sold the methadone to buy the heroin or ice. You would not think that purchasing a caravan park would complement your life's knowledge.

As time passes the confusion increases, the person should definitely not drive or operate motorised equipment. It's extremely difficult to say you cannot drive, specifically, while in denial. The discussion will lead to emotional outbursts. You will notice how behaviour will change, simple everyday tasks will stop, be incomplete or performed with risk. Touching electric utensils, trying to put a plug into a socket whilst holding the plug prongs was possibly a reality check for me with Katie.

The person that shows signs of anger, depression, sadness, loneliness and writing ability may deteriorate. The computer keyboard becomes a jigsaw puzzle, a book reader may lose the ability to communicate, read and or remember what page they had reached. They may have long-term memory retention whilst short-term activities or discussions are lost almost immediately.

It is more appropriate to have any specific discussions early in the day as Sundowning, dependant on the severity, will leave the person confused more than expected.

Anyone who knows anything about Alzheimer's will appreciate that phone calls after 4:00 pm will never achieve the desired result. And certainly, be it phone or conversation, never commit to dates, times, meetings etc. As the illness progresses it will not happen. Indeed, I have seen Katie convince me in terms of our conversation that all was being recorded; we arrived for lunch because she remembered who and where, she just got the month wrong. Of course, as the illness progresses you will receive no information, as everything discussed is lost.

I loved Runaway Bay, however, Katie did not. The problem was actually her, or should I say the illness. Loneliness, depression adaptation to new surroundings and circumstances are made more difficult. Emotions gradually diminish and the loving relationship over 50 years becomes a memory. Let's just say that the candle burns less brightly, as moments of intimacy become cold blank stares into space. The person, if allowed, will sit. If you ask, "penny for your thoughts" it's heartbreaking – they have none – none that can be realised that is. The vocabulary diminishes and they have difficulty finding the words and ultimately the words stop. When talking to counsellors you are assured 'that it is not you', it's normal and systematic to the illness. You ask carers in the same situation, who fully understand and the answer is always the same.

By the time we arrived in Queensland we had sought the very best in medical best practice however, as the Alzheimer's imbalance became more profound, we sought counsel from what was the Alzheimer's Australia, now Dementia Australia. Katie did not wish to participate – there was nothing wrong with her! Nor did our daughter but more of this subject later.

Katie agreed to: "just talk to someone," and you must remember this denial is after some years of specialist diagnosis, indeed the Medtronic shunt, none of which can be articulated.

I am not going to quote or discuss Dementia Australia as it is a well-researched organisation with highly skilled practitioners, numerous services and well-detailed information packages. This can lead a person as to how to seek initial diagnosis via the various Public Service Authorities such as ACAT, Aged Care, and Centrelink etc.

They will organise counselling sessions for individuals or families. We have involved ourselves as both individual and group counselling and they have been of immense value.

I will however at this state say that I believe the counsel/information sessions are of more support to the carer than the individual who has dementia, for the obvious reasons. As the illness progresses the person does not "take in the topics."

It definitely gives an outlet for carers to discuss their individual circumstance, easing frustration and stress. It also gives insight into personal experience in dealing with specific symptoms.

It is however not a caring ongoing daily support structure. It is a not for profit organisation, dependant on government funding for its continued growth. You are a statistic as indeed you are with other government services. Providers to the various publicly funded organisations are earning money from you or your spouse's illness and basically, that is all they are interested in. A recent example was $140.00 per hr for a care package, the cleaner paid $19.50, and I leave the reader to consider that.

I wrote to the Royal Commission into Aged Care about specifics. **Appendix 2. Royal Commission/Notation.** The real heroes of any of these organisations are the thousands and thousands of wonderful individuals who volunteer with no payment. We have found that these are indeed wonderful human beings who do care. To these persons, you are not a statistic but a person.

I make a personal comment about charities. If you have been running simple organisations in various communities (let's say sub-Sahara's regions) for 50 years and the status is now far worse than it was when you started – you have clearly failed. When in those years, despot dictators have syphoned off millions and millions into Swiss or Cayman accounts and the population is still starving, drinking filthy water, not achieving realistic education or medical standards, then you have failed. If the population of that country is totally dependent on charitable aid, then you have failed. Of course, the economic opportunist does not see it that way. They are only interested in their own wealth, irrespective of the suffering of millions. Mugabe was one such example of the corruptive nature of charity. It's no different to the UK, America or France selling military killing machines to both sides, either directly or otherwise. For example, both militaries of China and Zimbabwe control royalty wealth from minerals – enough said.

I would suggest a good deal of the repercussions have their roots in both the Lend-Lease and Marshal plans of Britain and the USA 1940s – early 50s. Ironically, they now criticise the 2013 initiative of Belt and Road. Hypocrites. The Romans, Spanish, French, British and then America, so why not the Chinese – it's their turn.

Louise and her partner Jen arrived whilst Sadie and John were visiting our new unit in Queensland when a situation developed, as usual, seen as my fault, traditional to Australians as I do not sit on a fence. I am not indecisive and I say what I believe. Many have a problem with that as a lie or melodrama appears to pervade everyday life. Specifically, social media. 2.5 billion controlled herding subscriptions addicted to the instruments developed. Portals which suck you in, whilst the creators walk away with billions in an extremely short time span in the digital/shared economy. When I initially assessed Facebook and its future negativity, it had 350,000 subscribers. At this point, I made the decision not to become part of the herd. Time will tell as Zuckerberg increases his billions. Time will show that the power this one individual controls, is not unlike persons like dictators in a different guise. Power corrupts, absolute power – you know the rest.

However, I make another point of a truly shared economy. All parties committing an old statement 'unity of common purpose'. I mentioned very early in my story the Canadians who came to this country to establish 'fast food operations'. One of those young men was Jack Cowin. Amongst other things, he started KFC in Western Australia and Hungry Jacks.

Early in my career, I was State Manager NSW for Jack. His wife came into the office with a copy of B.R.W. the rich list. She was 'proudly jocular, look at this, he is listed as worth $145 million and he wouldn't buy me a new kitchen, too tight'. Laughter. Jack Cowin is now reported to be worth a billion. That creation of wealth has taken him 50 years and with that time frame, this man has directly or indirectly given hundreds of people opportunities. He has created possibly millions of jobs in that time and whilst Jack is frugal (Packers comment not a penny more nor a penny less) he would have contributed millions to the economy. He is extremely generous, and whilst seeking financial opportunity, has supported many persons in developing new business opportunities.

Whilst one could comment as to the health properties of fast food, if bought to excess, I doubt whether anyone, as with social media, has committed suicide. How long have the modern disruptors taken to make billions – not very long and what have they put back? Very little.

It is possibly an opportune time to say something of Louise and a brief overview of circumstances:

As I originally stated she was given a Catholic school education, as was the wish of her nana and mother, and indeed, much to Katie's resistance I told her what I felt appropriate. That, as I was not Louise's biological father, I would tell her and that, if and when, she wanted to meet him. Katie would organise it. When it actually came time to tell her, it was for me a strange moment. It was a sort of 'so what? You're my dad' moment, now let's get on with life. She was over 11 years of age. Maybe a person knows inside, maybe she knew – I will never know. Her biological father had 'dumped' Katie. The family had shunned her (I actually brought certain members of blind faith back together in '76). She delivered Louise on her own after rejecting abortion, adoption and there was never any contact or offer of assistance, monetarily or emotionally from him. I have never met him, would not know what he looks like or his full name so I have only heard Katie's side of the story. However, any person of a realistic age who "runs" away from this form of responsibility has little respect from me. So maybe instinct came in and Louise knew, however when I told Louise life continued in the same manner as the previous 8 – 9 years. We had a loving relationship, supporting her in all things she wished to become involved in. At swimming she excelled; tennis extremely good, outdoor activity/camping, we did lots of it. Travel – I would often combine business and pleasure so she was exposed to flying extremely young. Good food and restaurants from a very early age as I had. She was just a normal child growing up in what I believed was a consistent, supporting environment. Lots of friends doing reasonably well at school. Then drugs intervened and insecurity took over. That commenced in her mid-teens. More later.

Our life continued with the return monthly visits back to Sydney for my injection and our little unit on the water. As Katie's health deteriorated so did my thoughts as to how long we could safely and practically enjoy the boating life.

Katie and I had studied boating and navigation in the early '80s and it had always been a joke (much to my annoyance) that she gained a 93% pass and I got 86%. She could do anything I could do, whether it was tripped into the harbour – the '88 celebration was a day on the harbour never to be forgotten. A memory of one particular incident that still brings back tears. We were cruising next to Ben Lexcen's boat surrounded by hundreds of boats running parallel to 'Coast Guard', the American training tall ship.

The sailors came out onto the mast rigging and pipe whistled a salute to Lexcen, a truly magnificent moment in life. As I was saying, to Katie radio, mooring, anchor etc. all came easily. As Alzheimer's progresses, coordination and spontaneity are diminished. Consequently, she started to lose the ability to tie specific knots and the ability to 'tie up' alongside wharves etc.

You notice that the gait deteriorates, indeed as part of any assessment, gait and balance will be regularly checked. It will deteriorate.

To this end, I was not able to have her go forward to drop neither anchor nor 'pick up a mooring'. We had an automatic anchor/bowsprit fitted, which meant I just dropped the pick from the flybridge. However, not so picking up a mooring in a southerly. Tying up at wharves becomes an art form for the over 65's – run out tide, high winds.

She started tying the boat up to the boat, not the boat to the wharf. Now, to those familiar with boating, many domestics occur, generally because of the pig-headed husband, in this case, me. Ropes around one or both shafts, anchor dragging (not enough rope out Phil – I know boats Katie, its okay! Bugger, the boats drifting) etc. All resolved at happy hour and other tales more hilarious. It is, however, no longer a joke when you realise that your best mate, literally could kill herself without really trying. I had by this time deteriorated in my own health with more side effects, sick and nausea periods and hot flushes. As a result, Prof. Gurney increased my medication to the next level at 90 ml of Somatuline/Lanreotide. This laid open the obvious if anything happened to me: fell overboard, had some form of turn, heart attack, now 68 years, what could Katie do? The honest answer is nothing. As with her symptoms, she could no longer use the radio, drop an anchor. Indeed, it was questionable, after many hours of repetitive instruction, if she would now even return the controls to neutral, let alone switch the motors off. If one looks at boating statistics – it is often the over 60-year-old, dead, as a result of a simple activity gone horribly wrong.

As we travelled, Katie started more pronounced incidences of incontinence. The new doctor, without much consideration, put her on Oxybutin – a fluid suppressant. I was not too impressed given her Frusimide intake to make her use the toilet. Reducing fluid build-up in various parts – specifically around the ankles. Incontinence will commence with occasional wet pants, an urgency to use the toilet, not making it and the associated issues. I started to carry spare knickers, dress, pants, towel etc. in the car, and while travelling overseas a backpack, with the spares for emergency procedures. The aircraft or train toilets are the most difficult to navigate and you need to ensure that others are aware of your intentions. Yet again, suspicion is around when you enter the toilet cubicle with a backpack. Many hilarious situations have happened on trains around Italy, when the police arrived to determine what this old pair of potential bombers was up to.

Greater suspicion ensued in Mexico and later China, the secret police and they are not as friendly as the Italians are. Well-meaning individuals who have no idea what they are talking about will advise you not to travel. Not so, you have however to be prepared for any eventuality. Remember that whilst your partner may have some form of dementia, they are not stupid, they may at this point understand and enjoy all that transpires on the holiday. They are just unable to articulate that experience. You, however, will be extremely busy organising for your loved one, so be prepared.

About this period, it was organised to have my injection in Queensland through a provider-assist based in Melbourne. That said, I was informed that the injection was costing in the region of $1,000. To me this is price gouging however, it was an income for the contract nurse. The injection process takes approx., 30 seconds. After quite some time of my injection routine, she advised me that this was the last visit, that the contract had been cancelled by assist and a new provider would commence injections. Disgusted, I cancelled the contract. It is interesting to note when you have cancer and your wife has Alzheimer's, it is a small comfort to get to know the particular person that gives the injection. It is given in a specific rear quadrant and if not given 'with care' it can hit the sciatica nerve – I assure you not a pleasant experience. I went to my local GP who advised that he would be happy to give the injection. I requested the cost and much to his surprise he said, "Why do you ask, it's a normal consultation, $70.00." From a, Not for Profit publicly funded government provider at $1,000 to Medicare at $70.00. However, it would not be long before the obvious next taxpayer rip-off occurred – later, GP bulk billed care plans.

Katie was clearly not happy in Queensland and we decided to move back to our second choice – Hawks Nest on the NSW north coast. I realise now that it actually made no difference, yet again, part of the illness, loneliness, leaving people you have known in Sydney for years and that is why you do not like your new home. It certainly depends on the depth of Alzheimer's specifically making new friends and acquaintances. As the person no longer has the capacity to hold a meaningful conversation with someone who has memory-related problems, it is meaningless going to social functions.

You are therefore confined to clubs and associations that may have similar people. The outcome of this, whilst meeting wonderful people, is shown in the following situation. We meet couples of which the women are all carers. Katie cannot find a bond with any of the women as they have their own difficulties dealing with their husband's problems. And of course, I cannot bond with any of the males because they cannot articulate. It's a very difficult situation and one cannot just make things happen. It, therefore, can become extremely lonely, especially if you do not have a family. We have met some wonderful people over the past few years; however, in our situation have found that if you are lucky to have tremendous neighbours, this balances the lifestyle. We have met unfortunate people, whereby both have some form of dementia and it can have devastating effects on what had been a long-standing relationship. In the case of a friend's parents, it split the family, sadly over the will amongst other things.

When Katie and I were both diagnosed with a potentially premature death we took out powers of attorney for each other. I would recommend to any person(s) without legal guardianship power, that they invest the time and money before not capable to do so. Or until such time that in the case of our friends were fighting over assets. It's not wise to suggest "it will not happen to us", our children will not fight! What about their partners, what if one son or daughter has a drug habit and is looking to use his mother or father's pension to obtain drugs? The sister has a normal lifestyle, however, afraid of her brother and stays away. The courts are awash with unnecessary disputes that could have been negated by Power of Attorney, Enduring Guardianship and Health care directives. We were told of some terrible outcomes, in particular how vindictive certain people could become.

When we sold in Sydney and whilst life was still realistic to our illness, we made the specific decision to get rid of all the 'stuff'. Many people hang on to things that in many instances are rubbish. One certainly realises that you have boxes and boxes of stuff that in most situations you didn't need; it was consumptive wants or is it their security blanket.

Our politicians tell us that under Keynesian economics we must engage a process of supply and demand, thereby keeping the economy 'booming'. Katie and I have preferred, and continue to live, extremely frugally believing that 'money' was better than debt. When you look at the younger generational groups who must have things now, even if it is bought on a credit card or debt, the diminishing equity in homes and length of payment times for mortgages and it is not surprising that no one wants your 'stuff'. You cannot sell your stuff because supply is saturated with the specific age group, we are part of. All doing the same thing – trying to get rid of stuff.

However, I do suggest that you have to make the break as your lifestyle diminishes and your time becomes more focused on your partner's health requirements. We have objectively downsized twice before this time in moving back south to Hawks Nest. Once more purposely making our material life less cluttered, more importantly movement around the home. The less cluttered and easy living that you can create the more will make things much easier as things become more difficult – if you see my point.

Each part of the journey will seem difficult; however, surprisingly it seems to get easier if you can create a routine for yourself as the carer. This does not always come easily and would often be orchestrated depending on your past work practice, your own temperament and any support you may receive. Katie and I have always shared tasks, although I always did the lawns and her the ironing. In our case, we are both reasonably well-organised individuals, which make the position much easier for both of us. Some people we have met definitely find the situation testing. Every situation is different, however, at diagnosis, the more preparation that can be done will certainly help in the latter stages. Because there is no option at this point to say, "It will not happen."

We moved back to Hawks Nest NSW, registering at a new GP facility. A rural/outback doctors' group providing the usual services. This set up another incidence of unsatisfactory circumstances whereby in our situation, our needs were not met and the 'system' does not rectify the associated problems. Once again constructively complain and you are blacklisted. Why? Because specific demographics in Australia do not complain, you are the oddball. The public service entities have all the appropriate procedures in place to deal with inadequacies, abuse of funding allocation, however, if one actually does 'complain' the problem is lost in the system, ultimately with nothing happening to remedy. Consequently, the problems magnifying, and subsequent overall standard decline.

Having worked in large workforce multi-site environs at the senior executive level, I saw a degradation of workforce participation in the latter part of my career. This was to a significant extent a number of factors:

- The strengthening short term, exit theories and 'greed' platform. Focused totally on maximising shareholder return whilst losing sight of the employee role, motivation, loyalty, community.
- The gradual move over three decades from full-time employment to casual part-time and as a result of the GST and subsequent ABN, contact employment. A reduction in real funding to both public service and private to ongoing training and development programs for employees.
- The greater influx of migrants – not speaking English and its associated problems with the workforce regards activity communicated requirements.
- An ongoing lowering of general educational standards. Inclusive of work experiences.
- A poor track record of senior management, development programs and outcome. And in my opinion the impossible task of hire, counsel and fire mentality in this country. Being extremely difficult to fire.

To my way of thinking, a great employee is one who knows that he or she can leave if they so desire yet chooses to stay because of their satisfaction level with the company, its employees, management, work environment and the ability to speak freely without consequence. They naturally appreciate that there must be a specific protocol. In certain corporations or organisations that may be exacting. Owing to the requirement of goods or service.

What one can find today is an employee that is often disillusioned and frustrated with management. In many instances locked in, totally demotivated and unproductive. Unable to find alternative employment, yet needs to keep this position to pay the credit card. Often in an environment, they are motivated to suggest what the "boss" (control freak) wants to hear. Top-down management direction, whilst the organisation is inflexible, unable to adapt quickly to market forces. Sadly, that was the environment that I encountered towards the very end of my career and whilst the root of the problems was with the Board and or senior management. It was in the next level down, and sadly quite often the woman that set this tone of the motivation and toxicity. Not because women are any better or worse. More that they are more likely to fill this level of authority and position without the appropriate training, falling short in leadership skills.

The same can be said of specific male ethnic groups who within their own cultural upbringing, place the dominant role over the female subservient. This was also undoubtedly inhibited or stopped the progress of many extremely competent women (and men) from reaching their full potential of leadership.

What has this to do with care plans? Everything and more, it's training, its regulations, its legalisation, pride in your workplace, world's best practice, its accountability, its good governance, its values, its respect – it's your upbringing.

You are clearly intended to have faith. More importantly, trust in your care and more specifically GP practitioners. Given your circumstances, at least you want to feel (even if not true) that you are an individual and you really matter. Not just a number with a claimed capacity or your number, which has a direct line of payment to their bank account.

We had not received a 'Care Plan' previously and agreed. What we did not realise, that in this instance, a signature (generally requested by the attending nurse) would result in the cost of this service being considerably more than our previous GP exposure. However, in this instance the service, care provision was less. The doctor did not wash his hands prior to or after giving my injection. An incontinence appointment, when they were running late, meant Katie, sitting in a corridor and wetting her pants. This is only a small number of unsatisfactory outcomes at more cost to the state. We subsequently changed doctors without comment and reversed back to the traditional doctor/patient relationship. I believe the instance of bulk billing could, and has, resulted in 'price gouging'. Specifically, when there is no real competitive option in remote locations. I am still waiting to hear from the business as to why we did not return and indeed given the complexity of our respective illness – how are we managing? Specifically, as we were on (a) the care plan and (b) my 28-day medication requirement. No doubt, I will be waiting a long time.

We now regularly visited the boat. Now in our seventies, we made another lifestyle decision, that to keep her we could become another statistic of, 'accident at sea' or worse. Material possessions since my early 30s have meant little, as long as I had a comfortable roof over my head, no debt and good health. My objectives had been principally met; she was however more than a material object. We had given nearly 10 years of care and attention to her every whim, a 'Savage' lady, small in stature, yet tough inside. Take the right path, and she would climb a mountain. To let her go is still one of the most difficult decisions to make, you can lose part of yourself. It's like driving a good car very quickly, some will break before the car.

As Katie's health continued its decline, the most common downside is a lack of engaging conversation and debate. In her case at this stage, she understood completely all that was being said and could follow the conversation with ease and intuitive reaction indicated agreement/disagreement, not so the verbal response. Words become more confused to a regular communicator. One learns to understand what the "words" mean. Ensuring a (to the outsider) successful interchange.

One appreciated the frustration that the person is experiencing, more obvious in persons with not such a good command of the language. We have noticed that a person with English as a second language, in an English-speaking environment, struggle far greater than others, further enhancing the frustration. This can easily be seen as aggression and a less caring intolerant outlook is not a good combination. Without question, the true nature of a relationship is brought to the fore through testing periods of relative hardship. Becoming one, yet having maintained individuality, means an easier transition to understanding what is being meant, lessening the frustration for the person. I personally despise the dumbing down lifestyle (un)reality programs that portray individuals in the worst possible environment of "lust", no wonder relationships do not last. Narcissism on steroids, males with limited brain capacity seeing a woman as purely an object of but one short-term opportunity.

Whilst a women's plastic breasts and pouting lips lower their feminine beauty to snare a looser. My wife is real from head to toe (except for a couple of bionics) and is still as beautiful without makeup today as she was 50 years ago.

No wonder our youth have inferior thoughts about body image and the associated social issues presently occurring within specific target market groupings.

Someone is making money out of them, certainly, Simon Cowell has. One nonetheless questions their ability in older age to care for someone. Indeed, if they have anyone to care for, they are selfish to the last.

Some have difficulty in dealing with the decline in cognitive reasoning and body functions. Gait is a definite marker, vertigo and vasovagal can lead to periods of dizziness and incontinence can raise its hand. Whilst we all react and cope differently, some are unable to do so and just walk. Bob Hawke was a perfect example, a self-confessed womaniser, a once heavy drinker and egotist. Hazel supported him through all his indiscretions and when she needed his support, he left. It begs the question, do different nationalities have different attributes to loyalty and longevity or is it simply your upbringing? Are Australians, particularly the younger generations, addicted to materialism, capitalism thereby denying loyalty and care? (50/50 Rule) Something that they will suffer dramatically as they too grow old and infirm, not so many Greek, Italian, Chinese and Japanese.

As dementia progresses, whilst not getting easier, I have personally learnt to adapt and believe have become a better carer. I will never know, one of the heartbreaking gut-wrenching side effects are the loss of appreciation or thanks. Indeed, as life progresses one wonders if the person cares, or knows as to what is being done for them. Standing in the bath picking excrement from the bottom after soiling the bed for the third time and yet another wash load in seven days. Rubbing it over the body, carefree and warm in the cascade of water. You shower her off, whilst cleaning the shower, wash the hair, switch off the taps. Drying her whilst utilising the prepared pile of clean clothes. Half dressed; you notice a dribble down the inside of the leg. Oblivious she is having a standing wee!

Washing her off, you change the previously fresh incontinence pants for new ones and dispatch the towels to the wash. You then brush the hair and show her how to remove her tooth plate, then how to brush her teeth and plate. It just becomes the routine – you will not change it and it gets worse, two, sometimes three times a day. In Katie's situation, incontinence has become an inconvenience, however, we (well I) have had to work around the problem: spare knickers, pants, towel and, as I stated earlier had had some crazy funny moments in our travels.

Determined to not allow the illness to restrict our retirement, Prof. Gurney had organised my script to be filled and then administered overseas. It would be another book volume describing the difficulty in navigating Public Service protocols: airlines, airports and customs with a pre-filled 120mg syringe needle with the substance being a 'gel' – think bomb. The only two airlines that replied to requests for onboard carry and chill facilities were Swissair and Singapore. The only countries' embassy to approve carrying the drug into their country was Switzerland and the United Kingdom. Its easy today, if they do not wish to commit, ignore the email. Accept a phone commitment at your peril. Consequently, navigating the globe has provided difficulty nonetheless we managed. Italy, Morocco, Spain, Hungary, Bahamas', USA, Cuba, Mexico, Sth Korea, Croatia, Singapore to mention a few during the course of four holidays – generally via Scotland.

Camel riding in the Atlas Mountains, Morocco. The camel driver was confused that the camel was 'leaking water' above the normal place of aperture. The captain's address to the passengers was halted on the Yangtze whilst we called a halt for toilet needs. Secret police kept a close watch as we navigated our way around various civic monuments – via the toilet. If you didn't laugh, heaven help. They say that "the home is where the heart is" specifically if you are a migrant, Scottish and have dementia. Katie's long-term old memory is extremely clear at this stage however, this leads to the loneliness dilemma – thinking back to your childhood memories and that of your family.

Without doubt, and as I have never hesitated in changing space if I were to suggest 'would you like to move back to Scotland' the answer would be yes, instantly, no hesitation. However, as with leaving Queensland, it would not remove the problem.

Now in 24/7 incontinence pants (known in the McLean household as knickers – not to confuse the removal with pants or jeans), we decided on a trip to China.

6) The China Challenge, Tangles and a Potentially Terminal Affair

This vast country had long intrigued us both. Its political history, commercial growth and until recent events 'unsung progress to a world superpower'. With all its reported problems (generally America), we have firmly believed for some 30 years that Australia's future lay in Asia – specifically China, Japan and Korea. If we consider, the loyalty shown to the UK by America, was only when it was (a) paid for by Keynes and Churchill – you fight the war and we will supply your total needs and (b) remunerated after Pearl Harbour eventuated. Does one really believe that America or indeed the UK would come to the military rescue of Australia if China took a military stance? I think not. Does anyone believe that with what military capacity we have that we can repel or invade? I think not. We should have been a major trading partner of China 30 years ago; as usual, we failed and continue to do so. It's all about volume and management competency, and we never seem to get there. Consequently, and considering the implication of incontinence, we decided to run the gauntlet and organised a holiday to China holiday via Scotland.

Scotland was great, much the same well-worn path – sees the outlaws, catch up on what was happening and so forth. China was something different, it made us remember our youth, industrial capitalism and pollution.

Both Katie and I have believed that the planet is undergoing a normal (or not normal depending on your point of view) transition in landmass, habitat and climate. That indeed, in some many billions of years we would evolve into another ice age and that we are definitely, as a species, having a significantly detrimental effect on our Home – Earth.

It took 200,000 years to reach 1 billion and then only 200 years to reach a population of 7.7 billion. China, in an Adam Smith flurry of supply and demand, proved to me that if we are to continue this male-dominated focus to power and war persistence, then we will not survive another 200,000 years, indeed maybe 200. We traversed some 9000 km by high-speed rail, road, plane and boat. Being left amazed by the scale of the infrastructure development, simply to satisfy 'world trade theory of stuff consumption', supporting the present and future population needs.

I was perplexed by the visual reality as to the magnitude of progress. Impressed by the open dialogue of the people we met, inclusive of the positive whilst oft arrogant attitude. Not unlike previous historical periods of power such as French, Spanish, British, American and Japanese, it was quite evident that:

- The general population are extremely hard-working (unlike (50/50 Rule) Australian, British, American) well educated with a good understanding of world affairs and historical impact.
- They did not mention the British or French, merely the colonialists, as such, they have had their industrial time, the Americans have had it (with double meaning) and now it's our time in history.
- They see India as a future growth corridor and that Belt and Road is simply strategic placement and mineral exploitation. Surely no different to past suitors of world dominance, both trade and military over the past 1000 years or so give or take a few years.
- Patriotic and extremely proud of what they have achieved and their dynastic history.
- The suggestion that the 'democratic model' would not work in such highly densified populations. Indeed, that democracy is weakening as populations grow.

While one considers the past 'I have a dream', and subsequent ongoing and present problems that Americans have created for African Americans, I find it intolerable that they, the Americans, can be so hypocritically arrogant regards Chinese ethnicity disputes. We found yearbooks to 2015 (the time of Xi Jinping's power push) and the data identified the reported size of funding for the specific scale of projects. Recent funding includes the world's largest Hedron Collider (2028) and a joint Chinese, Russian consortium to build an aircraft engine option to Rolls, Pratt & Whitney etc. (2026). It was the various statistics relevant to military growth and not only the ability to fight, but to win, that I found disconcerting. I do however believe that many are misinformed and as such make an inappropriate comment about China. Patriotism, no matter what Capitalism thinks of Communism and you have a potent ingredient for war or peace, dependant on how your attitude plays out.

This is the stark reality in the thinking of Xi Jinping:

- Absolute unquestioned power since Mao.
- The winding back of "freedoms"/open dialogue since Deng Xiaoping.
- The islands, Taiwan, Nth Korea, Vietnam and Indian territorial disputes.
- The Japanese: Yasukuni shrine and its symbolic gestures.

As Deng said in 1980, *"We must admit our deficiencies. We are a backward country and we need to learn from Japan."* The present leadership no longer holds that belief. It's a pity that Australian leadership have never learnt such humility.

- Tibet and the reported ethnic issues in the North West.
- Significant increases in a military capacity and spend. More so, international media presentation of power capability.

I was actually left thinking about male arrogance and indeed its history repeating itself. Specifically, the similarities to certain European happenings within the 1932-39 periods. The re indoctrination of the masses, military build-up and outwardly signs of power status. Disturbing when one considers that growth and capitalist prosperity had been built quietly (Deng) very much under the radar until now. As he said, "hiding the light, biding the time."

Indeed, when a country has succeeded so well without significant focus on military pursuits (until more recently), why not carry on that process of power by economics. By which time China would have well and truly surpassed the USA. Whilst Obama was cognitive about the Chinese, Japanese, American historical relationship structure, he appeared more Chamberlainistic than Eisenhowerish. Trump and his trade wars have indeed stepped up the struggle and indeed, it may well antagonise the Xi Jinping theory.

Quote: Politics is war without bloodshed, whilst war is politics with bloodshed. Mao.

Back to pollution. As we travelled, we observed mile upon mile of sustainable small acre farming, backed by similar levels of new growth forest – and pollution. New coal-fired power stations, factory after factory, and chimney after chimney. I am not suggesting that they are not investing in renewable, as we observed many signs of extensive wind and solar, more that they are not doing anything differently to others before them. That is, building an industrial and technological economic superpower by any means.

However, can this planet continue with past and present-day economic theory and the belief of future generational leaders (irrespective of nationality) that it is 'now our turn'? Specifically, if India and major Asian communities pursue the theory of supply, demand, associated consumerism and the impact impending upon 'scarcity and waste'.

What became incredibly surreal on this holiday, after years of travelling extensively, is this: the knowledge that if the rest of the planet follows the principles of present economic theory, we will not survive as a species.

Consequently, if we think that travelling to mars in a 'tin can hydrogen bomb' will be the start of a race to other galaxies and salvation we are merely thinking of investment shareholder opportunity, minerals; delusional at best, as to a travel mode. Whilst millions of the less fortunate die of starvation and wars and "world aid organisations" failed intervention, we have hardly celebrated "Adam Smith's Theory of Moral Sentiments" a good man and true! When all we embrace today is greed at any cost to humanity or the planet.

If Keynes were alive to review Lend Lease, Marshall Plans, level playing fields, free trade, and the world economy, I believe in looking at the state of the planet he would review his model theories, dramatically. I believe he would have evolved great theory. Having said that, would our universities of today, limited by public service thinking and mediocrity, not scholars, allow Bloomsbury? I doubt they would.

Theories are totally focused on materialism. In simple terms, everything is presumed to continual production of goods growth, with no consideration to the planets capacity to keep up supply without irreparable damage. Specifically, if we highlight the moral frailty of human nature, namely power and greed and its associated impact or growing inequality of wage and wealth distribution, the increased problems with waste, pollutants, population density, water security, agribusiness and wars, not to mention carbon tax, transferring a purported positive to a negative without actually eradicating the reason for the problem.

As you have read, I did not enjoy a learning period in school (totally my own fault and stupidity) so I do not suggest I have superior mathematical skills, nor an in-depth understanding of economic theory. Merely presenting my theories based on readings later in life, business exposure, travel and being simply an extremely concerned realist Australian tenant of planet earth.

We appear to have too many Professors, politically contrived system manipulators, rather than inspirational scholars. Not, in some instances, focused on creative thinking and mindset. Turing and computing, Turing and the war. One hundred and fifty brilliant mathematical minds and what do you create – Enigma, Smith, Dickens, Darwin, Einstein, Keats, Burns – we seem so lacking today. They all say the same today, daring not to challenge the system. No longer driven by determination and passion irrespective of detractors only their CV and pension.

We must develop a new Magna Carta, a new Wealth of Nations. Earth economics, the sustainable wealth of individuals and nations, by the restructure and maintenance of human dignity. We must 'wean future generations off excessive and unsustainable corruptive wants'. We must bring expectations into longer-term focus, not 'the now, the me' and minimise the expectation of modernity and stuff. We have to create moderation of mindset – before the war, famine or flood does it for us.

Stuff has become an addiction (50/50 Rule) to all consumers, at any cost. Stuff evades quality for quantity. A millstream throws away mentality in western structures and that decision pervading all life's aspects and aspirations. It gives a short cycle of purported pleasure or pain with no longer consideration to future implications. Poverty prevails. It does not make real relationships nor stop illness. The Power of Nations has become the Greed of Nations.

As Einstein famously stated: 'The significant problems we face cannot be solved at the same level of thinking we were at when we created them' to this end, the law of unintended consequences cannot be allowed to prevail. We cannot continue the process of creating new economic practices, intending to resolve in part and the original economic model that has created negative outcomes. What progressive, like a thinking person, would introduce mass gambling opportunity, knowing human nature that will ultimately create addictive response (50/50 Rule) and the social implications of mental and physical health? Whilst at the same time creating immense wealth for individuals (in Australia by way example the Ainsworth family) and institutional shareholders of businesses such as Coles and Woolworths. One cannot ignore the growth of an industry and the employment it creates. However, when the social, mental and medical costs to the community show consistent negativity over f decades, (A) why would you not consider the implication and make the recommended change and (B) then implement public service operatives that ultimately cost more in monetary terms than the income the first economic opportunity created.

Capitalism has taken away identity and individualism from the masses (the herd). It has taught us to more creatively lie and cheat. It has not evolved equality, and, whilst it has taken millions out of poverty, it has displaced and made homeless more millions. It has emphasised our arrogance more importantly reducing our compassion whilst highlighting our arrogance. It advances criminality on a scale previously not seen in history. It creates mind toxicity, annulling trust in leadership and partners. It stifles rational compromise, establishes fragmentation and highlights social cohesion. It maximises corruption.

Consider the disruptor syndrome. Take Facebook, that one individual and company has been allowed to create an instrument of control and subsequent power. We should have had alarm bells at 500,000 subscribers. Population 2019, 7.7 billion, knock off China 1.4, having its own portal and we have 6.3. Knock off 1.5 not connected and we have 4.8 billion and this company now controls 2.38 addicted subscriptions and growing, thank heavens he does not hate Jews!

Twitter arrived and I can never forget a comment on that day that Malcolm Turnbull made, something to the effect, "Standing at the No37 bus stop waiting to go into the city." My instant thought response was, "And he is a QC, heaven helps the herd." Who cares?

One recollects some years ago that Australia restricted the opportunity to become a QC believing that it could erode the significance of the position if it became so easy to attain, rightly maintaining superior legal judgement. I wonder if Twitter distorts any other legal interpretation?

My personal interpretation of the addictive mindset of what I will call: Facial Twitter.

Destructive, individualistic, hedonistic, illusionary, sociopathic, insincere, paranoia and shallow. The euphemistic misinformation. I prefer the statement: lies, lies and more lies.

Our trip to China was a wonderful experience worthy of a book, however, our respective health problems continued to deteriorate. Katie commenced double incontinence, walking, balance and distance issues. No one, unless reviewing our respective medical scans and tests, while looking at photographs, would think that we had anything other than older age synopsis. Note the front cover. Ordinary healthy oldies, how I wish. Consequently, it is difficult to have anyone – no matter how close, to understand. That today your "weariness" goes beyond tired, your stomach cramps have you relying on the toilet all day and your nausea symptoms have been so bad you just wanted to die – think chemotherapy if experienced. You do not want to consider that a forty-four-year-old, outwardly healthy businessman, (level 3) just died. If you look at his scans on his iPhone, you understand why. It does not make it any easier. One thing for sure: I cannot go before Katie. Who would care for her? No one. Maybe this is why some survive otherwise terminal illnesses. Maybe the mind is greater than the body.

'O wad some pow'r the giftie gie us, to see ousels as others see us.' Robert Burns

My breathing while bending down becomes more concerning, as though the body just stops and you zap back to reality gulping for air. As usual, the tests show nothing. 20% loss of lung capacity, smoked many years ago, not bad for a seventy-year-old Mr McLean. Of course, the Gallian 68 PET scan shows a different story. Your body is so slowly shutting down; thank heavens for medicinal new age pharmaceutical drugs and private health cover.

Quote, "All the years after 70 are a gift from the gods." Ye Zhikang.

A good theory in a communist state. I figure that 90 sounds better.

Not so illegal drugs. We discovered drug paraphernalia in Louise's toilet approximately at the age of 16, or should I say the cleaner found them, as we were generally banned from her domain. It was many years later that she told us that she had actually been able to obtain drugs (with the next-door neighbour's son) in the early '80s prior to our leaving Adelaide for Sydney.

Our relationship, both Katie and mine was difficult with her as she became extremely rebellious. We assumed that the aggression was a passing phase, typical of the teenage years, not appreciating that adolescent change and drugs are not a good mix. Both her mother and I had many arguments with her and indeed, over the years, there were periods of time that we saw little of her. Having independently moved out of the family home.

The relationship with her mother since her late teens had never been what one would call a traditional mother-daughter relationship. Going out together, friends, it never occurred. I was definitely unable to discuss rational options, as was Katie. You would get to a certain point in the conversation and, dependant on the mood, the shutters would close, as would any conversation.

When Louise commenced her periods, she was sent home and I was dispatched by Katie to leave the office (which was closer than hers was) to see if all was well. Apparently, they were not and the circumstances were discussed with her mother. As time progressed, she apparently had pains and heavy periods; this presumably led to similar problems to her mother and ultimately endometriosis. As with any topic, I know that Louise would never accept suggestions, which upset her mother greatly. In hindsight most probably the drug influence. Her drug habit continued and she and I had some arguments about that and her chosen sexuality. I said some things that I deeply regret. Having apologised, our life continued in the same mood swing and highs and lows tolerance. She had various partners and we became deeply concerned that she had no 'soul partner'. I had grown with a generation that did not understand or agree on a lesbian relationship. Nonetheless reading as much as possible on the subject, believing that I would rather see Louise happy with her sexual preference than unhappy in an unfulfilled relationship.

Katie has never accepted it, nor her long-term present partner, unfortunately, unlike me, Katie does not outwardly say or show it to others, only to me. I find this extremely frustrating and sad for Katie. After all, all she wanted to have was more children and subsequent grandchildren and which, if being completely honest, has depressed Katie as to her daughter's outcome. I accepted my daughter's sexuality many years ago and most certainly welcomed her partner with honestly and my usual opinion. It is therefore incredibly hurtful that by speaking my mind, stating optional consideration, whilst her mother despises everything about her daughter's lifestyle, too afraid to confront the situation. I think that I should mention that Lou has found a great partner. To her mother, no. Why not, because it's wrong.

Behavioural psychologists suggest we should never expect offspring from our children – tell that to Katie.

We sought professional advice from various behavioural psychologists over the years. As to how best to approach the subject of drugs and the questions were always the same.

- Does she have any problems in her life? We don't know, we cannot talk to her without an argument.
- Does she take recreational drugs? Yes.
- Later and more recently. Does she take drugs? We do not think so, or did she take drugs? Yes
- How long did she take drugs? Maybe 20 years.

The answer was always the same, "That the person has to want to change lifestyle, so our problems continued, never able to rationally discuss a topic." Start to dig deeper and the response was always the same, "Don't tell me what to do." On eggshells, that was it. Nothing changed.

We had always been immensely proud of her achieved independence by purchasing a home in Sydney on a single income. Going without to create, her strong work ethic, loyalty to friends, moderated lifestyle and no credit card.

She met a human resource executive with a major retailer, securing a position that she was not at that time ready for, nor had previous experience with. Given my background, it was quite clear what was happening and regrettably, a series of downgrades occurred. The relationship did not develop and of course, her mother and I could not help. And a mother that would never constructively criticise a subject, she is never allowed to. Too afraid to question her little lamb. Of course, Louise knows that and has played on the fact for years.

I believe that if she had had the capacity to listen to me, I may have been able to help. Yet again, no go, mood swings dictated my communication and quite possibly her employment environment.

She then met her present partner Jen, who had regrettably had a relationship breakdown, two lovely intelligent daughters and Louise had a quite common lesbian family relationship. I was delighted, not so Katie. Then we had our latest "spat" on the 24th of October 2015. The actual issue was overtaking a Colonel Sanders signed menu and not our (Katie and I) photograph from 1975. Also, her mother's difficulty in navigating a particular phone and that she should have an iPhone. My telling Louise that she did not know what she was talking about. Our first in-law's argument – far out! And McPartlin, only seeing one side (looking but not seeing) having the audacity to suggest, "Do you mind, we are on holiday!" Apparently, this is common practice, in-laws that is; I'm not used to it. All McLean are extremely honest with each other. Sadly, now all dead.

Louise and I have only spoken briefly once since, our only communication being emails. We have tried to engage her with options through dementia support groups. Nothing, would not discuss. We initiated further opinions as to her attitude and in particular the type of response as to my email comments. Reviewing my communicative style and her response from two independent professionals.

- Has she ever taken recreational drugs? Yes
- Does she presently take drugs? We do not think so.

In two instances, the opinion as to mood swings has been, "It could be bi-polar given the length of time she used. You would need to talk to her re medication." Talk to her? It would start a world war.

A more recent opinion by a GP was "could be Personality Disorder." I studied information regarding treatment symptoms of endometriosis and the hormonal treatment can indeed cause mood swings; however, who is to know, we could never discuss it. I firmly believe in the old statement 'that it takes two to tango' and appreciate that I am partially to blame in my cryptic comments. Notwithstanding the mood swings have been occurring for many years longer than the hormonal treatment.

If you can never achieve rational debate and discussion one must suggest, why to bother anymore. As a number of my emails detailed, "I cannot fight for your mother's health, my health, whilst continually fighting your mood swings."

The other aspect of my daughter's reaction was put forward by two behavioural individuals independently, that is: firstly, denial. Initially of her mother's symptoms, certainly, all the literature and role model examples I have experienced that it can be a significant influence on a person's attitude to the individual. More importantly, fear. In this instance, the condition known as familial that is where a person's family has a history of dementia – grandmother, mothers, aunts, which is the case in question. Subsequently, the fear that you may one day succumb to this dreadful illness. We have been offered counselling by various organisations, however, you need all parties present, and, as Louise had refused any involvement, I suspected that to broach the subject would create that third world war. We have in various seminars heard far worse stories from others, consequently one must try to remain positive. Again, social media has not helped, many thinking that they are in a play, melodrama at best.

I have always had a project in life. Generally, a boat, house investment fix up or later a rundown caravan park to fix. My career was a wonderful period of exposure and now I found myself with nothing to do. So, I reverted back to my lifelong passions, Demographic statistical profiles. This led me to a more philosophical thought process as opposed to a career-driven opportunity through profile knowledge. I then started thinking through the situation of obesity and the other links to lifestyle in a western capitalist democracy. As such consumptive addictive wants, stuff and waste. I am not suggesting that my theory has not been considered by many others before, indeed, considerably more intelligent and knowledgeable than myself. I am however suggesting that we must look at the topic in a totally different manner to that discussed and recommended previously. Hence my (50/50 Rule). 50 years of decline in the subject matter with 50% of the population holding that statistic or worse.

We must inspire our youth to forge change that in our mythologies to date that have failed. Take any subject: for example, plastic, in all its uses and consider one format, packing. In this instance food and retail packaging. The simple reason for its being is cost. As a bi-product, it has been relatively easy and cost-effective to produce. It is easy to manage, it gives convenience to consumers in pre-packed formats and it created hygienic shelf-life storage for both home, retailer and transportation, which is the supply chain logistics. However, it has all of the downside attributes that are now constantly profiled, damage to our ecosystems. Much has been said, much has been written, and nothing has been done.

We spend millions, indeed billions in creating new industries to solve the problems created by the original industry. My theory is therefore this; why not allow the old industry to die? Morphing into new thinking, whilst creating a new product(s) that enable cost-effective application at the same time enabling supply chain logistics? In the 1980s on a study tour as C.M.M. Coles Myer (Dept Stores) to Japan, Germany. The objective of the tour was to review Siemens Nixdorf Data capture and automated service logistics. One thing that has stayed profoundly in my mind to this day. Eating branded pre-packed products then eating the packaging. No doubt that idea was bought and subsequently bottom drawered. As a tyre industry colleague said, "We have bought many patents for tyres over the years Phil (think deforestation/think rubber/think burn-offs) that do not wear out. Have you ever bought any? No, for the obvious reasons.

Capitalism, consumption, power, greed, ecological degradation. Loss of habitat, indigenous home status, corruption, criminality, all for one product – rubber. We utilise a cheap slave labour product, short-term thinking, and long-term greed. Clearly, the average pig-headed male only lives to 74.5 years. Consequently, to his small brain, why would he care as to the disaster his generation create. That's the next generational problem. My conclusion as to issues outlined in my (50/50 Rule). If a problem persists and continues an unsatisfactory trajectory for 50 years – then we have failed. If you continue to create dialogue as to remedy – you have failed. If you can continue to implement new or recycled ideas or problems – you have failed. As a society, we have become complacent, looking for the easy option, not upsetting the status quo, as long as the wealthy continue their wealth. We are spending more and more time talking less time actioning. We have turned relatively simple solutions into mass propaganda and confusion.

Katie and I continued to attend various Dementia seminars, which further enhance the different issues that this dreadful disease proliferates. The information available highlights the outcomes from start to finish in the process of the journey. Indeed, one could suggest that Australia and the UK have possibly the best informative support and educational packages available. The forums allow discussion of specific problems often seen as your individual problem. After which, you realise that you are, as carers, all in the same situation, only at different stages of the relative symptoms. Incontinence appears as a common discussion point, double incompetence not so. In a particular meeting Bill, discussing within the group the difficulty dealing with his wife's toiletry problems, how in his situation he tackled the circumstances. Regularly pooping her pants anywhere, anytime with no medical solutions, that part of the brain closing down and not recognising what we take as a simple process of toiletry habit and action. Bill is a very gentle, quiet man and I certainly felt humbled that he would share this emotional period in his life. You later realise, as your own circumstances deteriorate, that in general terms, few will show that compassion and understanding unless they have experienced first-hand the dementia story. I did not realise at this stage, I would be dealing with this added burden to the daily dementia routine. That was to come. The largest hurdle that one initially experience is denial. The 2nd largest is convincing your partner to undergo the various tests and procedures. Subsequently, undertaking a forum group and its education. Determining with the stark reality that you may indeed be in the early stages. This occurred to one particular couple. The realisation that there is always someone with far greater difficulty than yourself.

Dr Google has not helped strength of character. I am informed that many under 30 years old are somewhat neurotic as to 'what may be medically wrong with them' Many appear totally focused on themselves and their daily 'struggles'. That they have little time for others. When given the statistical reality of relationship breakdown, single occupancy living and one appreciates the care at Federal cost requirement that will be expected in another 50 years. If we don't respect ourselves, how can we love and respect others? If we cannot keep our confidences in others, how do we create trust? If we don't have respect and trust, we will ultimately end in an extremely lonely life.

The dementia sufferer will become lonely. A novel is "stared at", not absorbing the words and ultimately the book is left on the table. The talking book has been rejected until it's too late. Concentration diminishes and the 'blank look' ensues. Looking into space "penny for your thoughts"? What do you mean? What were you thinking about? Your partner cannot answer so you improvise. You talk and talk and talk, hoping, praying that the stimulation will keep less cells from dying and you get varying degrees of response. Dependant on topic and day, talk about past enjoyments, hobbies, friends, music, travel. The response will gradually diminish, however, "the eyes are still bright" when you talk. The flame is still burning. Not so brightly while allowed to sit and stare.

Your routine is critical. Try to function to individual tasks one at a time. You find that if putting on a bra or sock, by way of example, you ask a question. "What would you like for dinner?" Two things will happen, the concentrated effort of putting the arm through the bra strap or lifting the left leg for the sock will fail and you will not receive an answer to your question. Lesson 1 – One task at a time. Keep to a routine of repetition. You are now long past the knives and forks in the cleaning cupboard or the plates on the TV shelf. You are now at "What is a knife and fork?" You eat with your knife and you watch as your cereal loaded to capacity on your dessert spoon falls down your clean blouse onto the floor. You will, however, just keep on oblivious to the situation.

I asked two experts was it right to tell (nicely and with consideration) the person to "do something?" Clean your teeth now become putting toothpaste on the brush, holding the brush over the basin whilst motioning to the mouth how to clean the teeth. The teeth will not get cleaned if you do not tell them what to do. The answer to my question was a unanimous yes. Telling people what to do for their own good, health and safety. Maybe if our authorities started telling the truth and started telling (50/50 Rule) people what to do we might see some improved outcomes. Tough love.

Wilf Jarvis a consultant behavioural change agent physiologist, told many stories. One, in particular, is that in raising children that they must know the boundaries. That no means no, and the tantrum in the supermarket will not result in lollies. Will on will. To know that no can be enforced by stop, don't do that and so forth. A child runs to the kerb and is told to stop, ignores the request, splat. The outcome of lack of discipline is an early death. Can we premise that to too much food consumption and the wrong type of medication, drugs, gambling, and domestic violence? We sure can. No boundaries are set by the appropriate mentors. Yes, sure it's equality. Sure, you have the right (or do you?). However, it's your responsibility and the outcome should also be yours. User pays.

"You are judged by what you do, not what you say you are long going to do." Kerry Packer.

We find with Dementia, that following a set routine the disruptors are reduced. Walking, without question in the early stages, maintains a more positive outlook. Indeed, you can notice small improvements in activity after walking, as opposed to 'I cannot be bothered' and reverting to just sitting. Obviously, the issue is oxygenation of the brain as walking stimulates the blood and oxygen to the brain. As the brain capacity diminishes, you will, unfortunately, find walking more and more difficult, specifically if gait and posture deteriorates. Your loved one will tend to spend longer and longer in bed. You are left thinking how you spent years trying to get her into bed, now you can't get her out. Getting the bra off, now you are spending your time putting it on. I find that a set routine helps me cope with the necessary workload repetition and ensures a simple procedure for Katie. I will tend to get up early, take her to the toilet. Change the pants if required and put her back to bed. The person will require more and more sleep and will suffer from greater Sundowning if they get up too early. I always set the next day's clothes up the night before. In our case, the days of discussing: 'What she wants to wear' has diminished.

I will prepare breakfast which is always one orange cut into segments, two types of cut-up fresh fruit, granola and Greek yoghurt, black tea no sugar. I make a note (50/50 Rule) that if every schoolchild, let alone the adult community were to have this recipe of breakfast prior to school, we would see significant improvement in productivity, learning, capacity and attitude. Not so a can of coke or similar and a slice of cold pizza. Take note young man (and woman), it is not good for your future health, let alone life expectancy. I will then tidy up, put a wash on if required and take time out to just think. I will then get Katie up, shower and dress her, recheck the bed, changing it if required and have breakfast together. I will then 'somehow' find out what she would like to do. We always make a point of doing something or going somewhere different at least twice a week. In Katie's case, she enjoys the drive. Of course, the direction, location and destination require toilet breaks consideration. You have to ask, as body language will not always indicate the need and it's almost an 'instant requirement'. A Niagara Falls pail into insignificance as to the density of flow and the flow is best directed to a toilet bowl than the car or train seat. The greatest distress is 'the tour'. Overseas and no toilet on the bus, instead of "are we there yet", is replaced with can you hang on to Shanghai. Finally, they find you a toilet and the sign, whilst in Chinese, Korean or Spanish, you know says the same thing as if in English – Closed for Repairs. You don't make the next one. You need to take care of the shopping. She has never been light-fingered till now, watch the small items, and whoosh! In the pocket. Or you miss the box of eggs as you finish your auto shop. Putting a pair of gloves on in Frasers Department Emporium, (it was cold in Edinburgh) and we walk out, making a speedy return when you realise that she does not actually own a pair of black leather types. The woollen mittens in her jacket pocket are hers. Your wife is now a serious criminal operative.

Meals – not easy. Enter eating establishment and play the usual recording, "do you need to go to the toilet dear?"

"No." You order your meal; it arrives and you take one mouthful as she stands up and announces to the restaurant, "I need the toilet." You take her, by which time your John Dory is as cold as the ocean it was caught from.

I look at what people now consume – takeaway, grazing, small snack, lunch, dinner, late breakfast or brunch and it's all the same – huge upsized quantity. Our fridges stuffed full with old out of date produce. Our cupboards bulging with stuff, often left to go stale. Purchased and unused on the little brat's supermarket whim, "I want it, mum." This should be replaced with, "Get lost, brat, you're too fat," or "you don't need it! Have an apple or pear."

Latest statistics, which are often cyclical: weather, season and price show that vegetables and fruit have declined in sales trending analysis. Snack, comfort nutritionally devoid products increased. If you don't have a clue as to supermarket schematics, just visit the confectionary aisle and take note of promotional items on special – 50% off $2.50. How can that be, it was $4.00 last week for a normal price, you are being fooled. Sadly, you don't appear to care, as long as it's cheap and easy for you.

A dear friend had a weight problem, which in turn was affecting his knees, unable to walk appropriate distance or exercise. Doctors prescribed all sorts of prescription medication, which, as in most instances, made matters worse. Discussing the issue (and he is an intelligent, generally sensible person) we were talking about his usual diet. In short, he appeared to eat a healthy diet. Limited serves at 90-gram meat and fish options, an appropriate vegetable range, pasta, salads, and no processed meat, as scripted in any decent diet book outline requirements. "I really eat very little Phil and there is no reason why I would be so overweight, 6'0", 22 stone." A disaster waiting to happen, heart, diabetics, you name it. Drinks little alcohol, does not smoke. Consequently, let's ask the real questions. Do you take sugar? – Yes. How many spoons per day? 5-6, but that's all right I have always had a sweet tooth? Do you drink Coca Cola or similar syrup/carbonated energy/soft drinks? Yes. 2 x 1.5-litre bottles per day. That's the equivalent of 25 spoonfuls of sugar per day. But it says, "No sugar," added Phil. Yes, it's a sugar substitute. Sweet biscuits? Yes. Crisps? – Yes. Dare I ask doughnuts? Yes. Do you eat every day? – Yes. Well, my dear old friend, you have been conned. Like an alcoholic, you are addicted to sweet sugary things. 63% of the national population are grossly overweight. Queensland is the worst state and the data statistical trending is deeply concerning (50/50 Rule)

- We are becoming lazier and consequently, our productivity is one of the worse on the planet.
- We continue to increase our 'sick days'. Friday or Monday. We have lots of colds and we continually feel tired.
- We are continually being told, "How wonderful we are." Well, unfortunately, that is not as others see us overseas.

The arrogant loudmouth uncouth American in the 70 to '80s. The cruise ship, the airport bar, the tourist resort – the French or Israel in the '90s and by 2010, the nationality had been replaced. Yes, you guessed it. It's now a drunken foul-mouthed Australian (50/50 Rule) over 50% drinking regularly to excess. And of course, like obesity having grown up with. Believing it acceptable. Grandfather did it, father did it. At 46 years of age thinking that, this is normal. The blokey, bloke thing, first to punch last to think. Tough exterior yet weak in mind and potentially alcohol-related dementia. Wernicke – Korsakoff's syndrome being an option that these people may look forward to. Irrespective of all other mental and medical options open to them.

Many years ago, I smoked, as did many of my generation. As with certain foods, alcohol, illegal and prescription drugs they can become addictive.

At 25 or 26, I went to the doctor. He said: "do you want to live to 50, to see your children, have grandchildren, enjoy life etc.?" Of course, I do for heaven's sake. Well, stop smoking otherwise, you won't. Cold turkey was not easy, failed twice, however, succeeded. Now that was a truly wonderful human being and doctor. No bulldust, no concern for today's litigious society. Simply straight-out honesty, it's your choice. Live well or die young. Oh sure, I hear all my critics "but my grandfather smoked and drank all his life and he lived till he was 92." Guess what, he was bloody lucky, a statistical minority – you may not be as lucky. And I would offer for consideration that our gene pool is being degraded. Politicians and the controlling moneymen. The industries that create an economic opportunity for all its worth. No political will to make the tough decision. One gets wealthy, one secures a good pension and one dies. We can do better than these people, we have the intellect, we have the knowledge, and we just have to become tougher, with ourselves.

With Katie's routine, I find that if you can second-guess activities, needs or wants it helps with her comfort. You need to remove distractions that may, to her, suggest the wrong time of day or night. For example, if you lay the clothes out for the next day in full view, let's say on the bedroom chair, and you take her to the toilet at 2:00 am and ask her to go back to bed whilst you use the toilet, by the time you get to the bedroom she will be getting dressed into the clean clothes, over her nightie. When you have long been the cook (thank heavens for my early career background), launderer, cleaner and dresser you will reach a point when you have to first help, then totally support; hair, wash and brush, cleaning teeth, toothpaste on the brush, showing how to hold and use the brush whilst removing/replacement of denture.

Early I mentioned Bill, who, as a carer had all of the associated problems. However, in his situation, his wife having double incontinence. Inconceivable, could this happen to us? Well, it finally did. The worst nightmare realised.

I have never been good with faeces (or vomit), and, whilst sharing all child growing up responsibility, I was not too good in the nappy department or indeed to a lesser degree carsickness. I guess we all have a weakness. Mine is you know what? I would certainly have never made homosexual. My stomach churns, I want to be physically sick and here I am with my best mate 'pooping' her pants, whilst not realising she has done it.

So, this is the real world and like anything else in life you just have to 'rise to the occasion' as my grandmother would say, get on with it.

We seek all the appropriate medical/care/dementia advice and you find but one thing, there is nothing anyone can do, it's part of the journey. Total agreement, no one likes this process. Thank heavens for that, I am bloody normal.

You hand the toilet paper, pre-folded, the bottom is wiped through the vagina. No, you won't change it. That part of the brain is now dead. You ask your soul mate to "put the paper in the toilet", "Just put it in the toilet dear, no, no don't fold it; no, it's got stuff on it. Please just drop it in the toilet. No (voice raising) no, not on the floor! Please just put it in the toilet." Thank the stars she only does a no. 2 once a day. Phew. We can now relax. Am I making it worse? Maybe I'm becoming paranoid about excrement. I say Kenny and I thought that funny.

Each period of the journey is the worst, or so you think. Believing that it cannot deteriorate further, that this is it. You get better, you learn to adapt even to become more and more tolerant. You don't get frustrated and you are winning. This is fine, we can handle this, wonderful. Wrong. The next step on the ladder and another symptom creep into being and you're on the floor. Wham! Start again Phil, get climbing. Heavens you are only halfway up the ladder now. The glass is still half-full.

"You didn't cancel the appointment."

"What appointment dear?"

"The dentist."

"No, that's on Wednesday at 12:45." Over the next three hours, (it's now 1:30 pm); she asks five times what time we are leaving for the dentist, twice getting up from the chair to leave. Five times, "No dear, it's on Wednesday at 12:45, today is Monday, and we have another two days before your dental appointment."

During dinner, at 6:30 pm, "We need to hurry or we will be late for the appointment."

"What appointment dear?"

"That appointment."

"What one is that?"

"At the shops."

"Do you mean the dentist?"

"Yes."

We get ready for bed; I help her clean her teeth. Get into bed. Switch off the light. "Good night, dear, are you warm enough? Did you cancel the appointment?" I lay quietly crying into my pillow. My heart is breaking. The "books" tell you to go along with the charade to go along with the hallucination. The image of her sister. "When will Hannah be here?"

"She should get here later."

"What time?"

"Maybe around 4:00 pm."

"How is she?"

"She is fine dear." You pray she does not ask again, Hannah died two years ago. We went to Spain to see her. We missed her by three weeks. You buy more shares in Kleenex.

Since my argument with Louise, I have only seen her once. Very little was said. As lately, the only communication has been emails (by her and me) and her weekly obligatory phone call to her mother, traditionally after 4:30 pm, the worst time to call. Ignoring requests to seek advice read the applicable dementia study sheets or indeed have her mother stay with her for a few days. Nil since October 2015. She has visited her mother 20 times, inclusive of the times that I would drop her mother at a meeting place when we travelled to Sydney. In those visits seeing her mother, the longest time being three hours, the shortest 1.5 hours, total 37 hours in four years.

In discussion with counsellors as previously stated. Is she on drugs? Never once has she offered to take her mother away for a few days. Give me a break. All she can do is email, "Phone not switched on." Dementia Australia said, "Just switch the phone off." It's not worth the problems to you. I have long given up on me. However, I will never ever forgive her for what she has done to her mother. Years of drugs – don't tell me what to do. An emotional barrier, don't let anyone in. She has failed her mother abysmally and she knows it. Is she afraid of the possibilities? If she hates me for saying what I think, if I am completely wrong, if I totally caused this impasse – she has still failed her mother. I will go to my grave knowing that I did do, to the best of my ability, and at times failing, never ever let my wife down in her most difficult state in life.

Louise will go to her grave knowing in her heart that she failed. Both herself and her mother.

Maybe it's the western democratisation of the herd, the dumbing down melodrama of unreality TV and social media, the press's reporting the day and the drama. R.S.V.P. soon forgotten. Disruptive thinking, political lies and spins, our insensitivity, all caring, and no care.

Our youth becoming 'C' grade actors, playing out (un)reality theory. A game of golf, of course, I can beat Greg Norman. A jet fighter action hero, of course, I won. I am the greatest. My parents told me, my teacher told me and the government told me. I can be anything I want. Equality, we are all equal. What a let-down if you realise that you are just another little 17-year-old shit, as I was with a lot of growing up to do. Your parents give you everything (bloody stupid parents). Your Nan and Gran spoilt you rotten because your mother was a heroin addict and you never met your father. He was just one of many "partners" and all we think about is balancing the budget. Continual economic theory. Maybe that's the problem with my daughter, she is trapped.

Quote, "the day is not far off when the economic problem will take back seat, where it belongs and the arena of the heart and head will be occupied where it belongs or reoccupied by our real problems. The problems of life and human relations, of creation and behaviour and religion." Keynes J.M.

Please excuse me, I hear Katie. It's 9:45 am as I enter the bedroom, it stinks and here she stands in a pile of excrement, the bed covered. We retreat to the shower, clean up the incident, make the bed, another two washing machine loads. We have breakfast, not a word spoken of the incident. It's just the start of another day. God, I forget to switch the phone on. Hell, another email from Louise, "Phone not switched on." Heavens I upset her schedule!

"A difficult journey walked is best not walked alone."
McLean P.C. 2016.

We as a western synergy are engrossed in consumption. We are too fat, we gamble too much, we rely on prescription or illegal drugs and we have failed relationships. We flaunt our worst paranoia, TV reality shows, local media, Twitter and we think we are bloody wonderful. We are narcissistic, photogenic seeking, shallow and boring. We pretend to care whilst it suits.

What a shame that we actually do not give a damn. We have been conned by lies, deceit. Politicians and Oligarchs, hedge funds and capitalists. Whilst they have created their wealth, our debt has proliferated. Our soul has shrunk and our fight has waned. We are complacent and soft. We have forgotten: "United we stand divided we fall." We have lost all moral compasses (50/50 Rule).

One of my most respected individuals in our police. Every day on the beat Cop so to speak. How do you think they feel, and we should, when I give you a statistic that is not (50/50 Rule)? Please note: 43% of males under 40 years of age have a criminal record for some form of alcohol or drug-related incident. 43%.

This is what the rank and file understand. They deal with the aftermath, day in, day out. Whilst their top brass play politics, glossing out the reality. Making continual excuses for the system, playing the politician of the days. As things continue to deteriorate. Leave drugs alone, it reduces other crime stats.

We must start and take serious note; we must re-emerge as masters of our own destiny. A politician will never help you. History shows us that. Who has continually taken us to war? Who allowed disruptors to prosper? Who failed to act on critical elements? Who became a despot? Who created genocide, who allows military weapons in mainstream populations? Who continues to allow drug proliferation? Who overseas continued increases in domestic violence? Who continues to grow and mismanage their fiscal responsibility of the public service? Who takes months or years to make critical decisions? Who quashes free speech? The list goes on. History repeating itself over and over again. Who ignores policy advice year after year? (50/50 Rule). Addictions: obesity, medications, illegal drugs, gambling, domestic violence, relationship breakdown. Who talks incessantly but never acts? When you travel to superb European destination cities, when you don't find bottle shops on every corner. Where you can't find poker machines (not that I would want to). Where the place is alive with tourism. Where the streets are safe. Where cafes and pubs don't stay open all night, and the money is flowing in. Young people enjoying life, happy, contented and not 'off their face'. Then you come back to Sydney. Take a walk around any night-time pub area at 4:00 am. Watch them spew, wee or slump in doorways, laneways, it's all on show. As our real people tourism diminishes as we attract party animals.

Take Coogee Bay or Dee Why or the Cross, I was asked by State and Regional Development to look at a number of businesses in the late '90s. Bakery/patisserie and I needed a very early start. Talking to locals about other businesses in the area. Heroin on the first floor, children on the second floor, transvestite to the rear. The wall in William St. young Asian boys selling sex. And then it's 4:00 am and the herd emerge, semi-human alcohol, drugs or both. Just ask a taxi driver, ask the cop or the 'ambo'. Don't ask a politician they are too interested in the economy, balancing the budget – not the sole. My reports were unheard of.

Blurring the lines, we have now "lumped all elements" into mental health. Eases the statistical reality. Not drugs, ice, cocaine, or alcohol abuse etc., its mental health. We create sub-diffusion, make the problem look less problematic. It might resolve itself; I only have a four-year term then it will be someone else's problem. The government and its ministers are surrounded and supported by an army of incredibly skilled, highly intelligent and specialist research advisory individuals and groups. Any C.E.O. would give his or her right leg for this level of advice, data and succinct précis of a given situation. Creative, original, confirmation of previous, advice. So, what is the problem one would ask? A manager enacts. A leader acts. Politicians do nothing.

How many years does it take to be decisive? They don't even have to think, the answers are provided for them. Life is about options; the future is the right option. The right option is rarely the easy option.

One could ask one simple question. The one I would ask – let's just take for example gambling. However, the same principle applies to all other aspects of the (50/50 Rule), and of course many, many others.

Gambling, over 50% of the population with addiction. The associated social and mental health outcomes, criminality and corruption. Around $800.00 per week for every man, woman and child. Pretty bad!

50 years. You first ask for a synopsis of all recorded material, data, submissions, reports on the topic filled away over the past 50 years. You give the information to your best five PhD research persons. You tell them your objective: In10 pages, from all the information sources, give a statement of the overall findings, its options, its recommendations (inclusive of a common theme/finding) and as such a two-paragraph statement of recommendations of all social, medical and environmental/economic implication, in that order.

Thereby based on 50 years of expert (ignored) recommendations. It would happen. End of story.

Have you ever sat on a committee? Have you noticed how generally two people will take charge, there will be factions, in all too many situations the initial objective will be forgotten and an outcome will be long in coming? Is this democracy? Or is this the democratisation of indecision? I offer a little example. A major Australian retailer, billions of dollars in sales, thousands of employees, the future and security of individuals and the move to change signature, a new uniform is needed and the decision outcome is given to a committee. After 12 months of infighting, nastiness, indecision, emotion, no decision had been made. This is our democracy; this is our parliamentarians and as such we now have (50/50 Rule) heading for 60/60 if we continue as we are. In most instances the answers are already there, awaiting positive action. 500 or 5000 brains better than one.

Life has many stories. Singapore, Managing Director, and Chinese, of a major Malayan Corporation, my question: How does your capitalist mindset work? Answer – take a good or service, find somewhere that it doesn't exist, implement it quickly and quietly.

Quote, "Hide its light and bide its time – with humanity? Not war." Deng Xiaoping.

Politicians are the real disruptors. Their personal light burns brightly in their own ego, it burns out quickly as their indecision quells their fire. We have had enough reports, submissions and recommendations looking for a simple solution. The answer has been there for 50 years 'Keep It Simple Stupid' (K.I.S.S). Just get on and do it. Make a bloody decision and don't wait for your lawyer to make it for you. You would never make any. My apologies Adam, John and Chris.

How many ideas, concepts, recommendations, advisory groups, committees have been written or convened over 50 years? How many replicate initiatives are conducted in other countries? How many projects have been stalled or cancelled only to be completed years later at three times the original cost, only to find that another new project is required due to the time lag of the original? How many projects have been rushed through to satisfy a political agenda to find 10 years later it is not satisfactory for the long haul? How much we may ask has been squandered, wasted, and lost? Monies that could have been used for education, medical, law enforcement. No doubt, the waste is billions. The funding is not the problem, it is how those funds are mismanaged. That is the problem. Ministers are answerable to no one because 50% (50/50 Rule) of the population do not question. They have been squashed, dumbed-down, manipulated, ignored and threatened. As such, that ultimately their desire has diminished. Why bother? What's the point? No one listens to me. Twitter and the like have actually taken the sting out of the tail. It's created a forum, a statement of mistrust, confusion, nothingness. Certainly, it has not created robust debate, it pits good against bad. It creates media fodder; it certainly does not stir action for positive change. The dumbing democratisation of the herd. The castration of opinion, reason and decision. That's America, that's Britain and sadly that's very much Australian.

Could you for one moment consider a revelation, a second wish? The first being "weapons to dust" however, whilst far more realistic – still most likely as impossible.

The scene goes something like this: The PM calls the opposition leader, "We have to talk I do not care how long it takes this is critical to the future of this country." The meeting convenes the basic principle, that the two men with their senior ministers will form a complete coalition for a given period, hold talks and with the subsequent recommendations, completed (50/50 Rule) agree on the 20 key elements agreed for implementation in this first phase of the re-born Government thinking. Then, and only then, advise the strategies and totally focused, get on with it, irrespective of critical comment. And there will be much. Our mindset has become framed to criticism and negativity more than would be expected of a vibrant cohesive society. We must bring back the trust in leadership irrespective of opinion, disagreement or polls. We prune heavily to create both form and beauty. It nonetheless looks awful in its creation. Cut, grow and blossom.

We all grow older differently. Mine has been to ensure that I leave some form of constructive mark. I do not write often. However, when I do, I give my opinion considerable thought and reflection. I believe many of us feel exactly the same. Reasoning emotion as to specific circumstances. I wonder often why is it that many 'retired politicians' suddenly see the light and no longer appear to speak with a forked tongue.

What the public desires of politicians are honesty, decision, empathy and understanding, notwithstanding, improvement and balance in the lifestyle of the population.

In Tony Abbott's ultimate downfall, he is reported to have said:

"The real problem with political life today was the careerism and the incessant desire to rise to the top. Subtly and slowly over time, you lose your ideals in the pursuit of the position. When you get to the position you turn out to be no good because you have sold out."

Why does this happen now? Why do the former antagonists proffer elder statesman presence? Why not listen to your conscience in the first place? Not your ego.

Chambers 1901 states: "Politician, one vessel in or devoted to politics; a man of cunning." Maybe that's the problem. Or maybe more. Macquarie 1981 states: "A seeker or holder of public office who is more concerned to win favour or to retain power than to maintain principles. One who seeks power or advancement within an organisation by unscrupulous or dishonest means."

So, is this what Tony Abbott meant? The Great Charter, the Magna Carter created a vehicle that grew from factionalism, fighting and marginalisation of the masses into the Westminster principle and separation of powers. Maybe we are entering the full circle and self-destruction. We are certainly not in a good space. One thing is however clearly obvious. We cannot continue in the present direction if our species is to survive the planets status change.

- *Evolution to the next ice age and the human-made present implications of global warming.*
- *The impracticality of all forms of present infrastructure for future survival.*
- *Mass annihilation or individualised wars.*
- *Water security and clarity.*
- *Present methodology to agribusiness – health implications, starvation and land degradation.*
- *De forestation*
- *International drug trafficking and its impact upon social welfare, criminality and social disorder.*
- *Capitalist inequality and the breakdown of social structure and rogue markets.*

Dementia has many undesirous consequences, not unlike politics, pollution and waste. The deeply disturbing situation is that at this point in time we can do little about dementia. The brain function slowly deteriorates, ultimately dying before the body and its associated functions. It is polluted with toxins and ensuring problems create waste.

Think incontinence pants or indeed nappies for babies. We no longer wash a nappy. We use the disposable method of using resources and creating waste and pollution.

However, this should not be so. As a species, we have proven our ability to adapt. We have shown moments of creative brilliance. Our youth at times excel. Consider the depth of skill now coming out of China, India and Japan. My belief is that we will ultimately source a cure for dementia and politics. It will nonetheless require great depth of collaborative thinking and action by a new breed of human. Those that no longer are prepared to suffer as a result of previous generations of previous neglect, inaction, bureaucracy, corruption and inequality. Those that are no longer prepared to sit back and let life and opportunities pass by. A new age determined by agility, reason, philosophy and moderation. That generation will have to re-establish self-worth, independence, integrity and 'we-ness" not "me-ness'.

You cannot continually sit astride the fence. Trying to be all things to all people, eventually, you will fall off.

As dementia progresses you realise, given in this instance my own health situation, that you will require assistance. There is a point that a carer will possibly require assistance with toiletry and other activities. These procedures will be dependent on your own stature, health and cognitive capacity. A 55kg lady is hardly able to manage a 95kg husband, father, brother etc. with specific tasks. Just dressing a person, maintaining their personal hygiene and that of the home becomes a difficulty relevant to the circumstances. Consider meal times. If you wish to maintain a quality appropriate regime then you will have to consider: shop, prep, cook, clean and as the illness progresses, help with the physical nature of eating. The type of food and preparation will dictate the ease with which your loved one will be able to eat. Cutting up meats for example. Katie may now try to use the knife 'upside-down' or the fork may be in the right hand/knife in the left, all totally out of character. I find that it is far easier for her if one covers one procedure at a time. For example, if you placed in Katie's case, her medication and water, orange segments and a bowl of fruit/yoghurt in front of her for breakfast, she will become confused as to what to do. Maybe pick up the medication in one hand whilst trying to eat something with the other. Whereas if you do each step individually, she appears to find the process much easier. You may ask her to take her medication three or four times, whilst she will tell you she has taken it, you have to ensure that tablets are not on the floor. What I guess, I am trying to say is that as the illness progresses you cannot take anything for granted. We have hilarious routines with going to bed. Whilst it's treated as total fun, no doubt as with all activities they sadly eventually become problematic. In this instance as simple as it sounds, Katie will get into bed 'the wrong way around'. That is, getting in, turning around with her feet than on the pillow or lying across the bed. You may notice that this posture in the chair, bed or car seat will start to replicate the foetal position.

As time moves on, your partner will stay in bed longer, indeed in many instances, I am advised it is better to let them sleep to a certain time. If for example, I woke Katie at 8:00 am (she used to leave for work at 6:45 am for years and years), the day would be more problematic for her specifically if we were to go somewhere. She would be far more incoherent and confused in the general morning activities, however, I find that if I wake at say 5:30 am, take her to the toilet (A) being selfish, I will not have to change the bed and (B) she will be more her 'old self' when getting up. Happier, better body language. The main focus for me is her wellbeing. Simply in that as I stated earlier you can never take anything for granted. Leave her for 10 minutes to answer the door and you cannot assume that she will have finished dressing. Even though you have laid clothes out. You leave for the door, it is cold upstairs and at this stage, she has on her bra, knickers and thermal top. When you get back, she has on one sock, the jeans are inside out and the buckle on her shoes have been put together, but not on the feet and she has no top on so now is getting cold. Get the idea?

'Love is a serious mental disease.' Plato

As I mentioned earlier the 'care plan' that a specific GP instigated was simply an exercise in his future care, not ours. I would make note we now have a wonderful GP in a tremendous practice and we chose not to be on a care plan. We applied for ACAT and Katie was accepted for permanent care when required.

During the process of agreeing on the appropriate outcomes, we experienced the bureaucracy of our public service mentality. Rather than detail by detail the circumstances that we experienced, I have submitted our letter to the Royal Commissioner and the subsequent response**. Appendix 2. Royal Commission/Notation**. I believe that this highlights my point of appreciating that the specifics were not part of the guidelines.

You would have by now realised that I abhor bureaucracy, hierarchal autocracy at that. About the only country in the world worse than Australia is India. A great country whose opportunity and progress has been hindered by politics, corruption and bureaucracy. Very sad, lovely people.

There is an economic term. X inefficiency. Simply that for example, inefficiencies in work, organisation, overstaffing, and demarcation occur in the coordination of inefficient deployment and management of resources arising as a result of bureaucratic rigidity and lack of competition.

You would note the point I refer to the front of house/back of the house in my report to the Commissioners. The Public Service has proven for years it is not capable of operating business structures effectively. It creates Fiefdoms. 'Peters Principle'. The promotion of an individual above the level of their own competence more interested in a 'clean CV' and power than the practical outcomes and total efficiency of the organisation. Simply, the size of a given budget, number of employees/reports and the complexity and nature of the business and we might see an executive paid a salary at some $500 or $600,000.00 per career public servant. The expansionary agile competitive private company with a similar budget, workforce and complexity with executive international search may well accede a salary of 8 to 10M with bonus plans.

You generally get what you pay for. The crux of the problem is that Australians are not stupid. We have all had dreadful experiences with bureaucracies for many years and sadly, we have 'given up'. As we hear too often, "it's the system." Guess what, it's not the system? It's the people that create and operate the system that amasses inefficiency. How many public servants have you heard complaining about their workplace? Low morale. Always a criticism of the 'bosses'. You are a product of your environment and too frequently, your work output, ethic, manner, enthusiasm and achievement will be governed by others within the workplace. Indeed, the home, school qualifies for the same comment. If your workplace is covered by autocracy and you accept it, it's a job. Then in time, if 'a pension survivor' you will quite possibly emulate those retaining power and promotion without consideration for the alternative, thereby continuing the system.

The alternative is wonderful. Very early in my career, working for Canadians, I experienced a management style that set my course as to 'what can be achieved'. One simple instance working with a management consultancy group and Graeme Straughan. To determine and then implement new and appropriate business/operational methodology and standards. It set a pattern of style that lasted until retirement. Involvement, acknowledgement, consultative, decisive and straightforward. Your people must own the idea. You must be prepared to accept criticism and you have to listen, not just talk, the cook, the cleaner, the receptionist or the maintenance person, to name a few are just as important as the GM, indeed you will more often find the "real issues" within the organisation from these people than you will from line management, divisional heads etc.

Respect is earned, it's not a title and making well communicated tough decisions for the good of the organisation and employees (not the stakeholders) will ultimately create respect. Indeed, research after research over many years has proven that a CEO concentrated on "the business" creates greater yields/ R.O.T. and shareholder wealth than organisations that focus totally on the share price/dividend. Whilst many would argue, I prefer the private model, creating both wealth, employment and community with politically less greed and subsequent inequality if managed appropriately.

That has however been a tough ask in the past 30 years with the manipulation of the masses by a few. No doubt, Soris would disagree.

Trust and honesty, apparently lacking in spades now, has evolved into mistrust and dishonesty. Many fear speaking the truth. The legal system has not helped this cause. Given a fair trial has become 'get off at any cost'. Plea bargaining, manipulation of the jury, inconsistent or inappropriate sentencing in criminal law. Ineffective legal public service watchdog entities. Authorities that continually ignore their own codes with eventual consequences. The building codes are a perfect example, covered by the press today as a result of totally unacceptable building standards and practise over many years.

I remember an instance, one of many, when clearing Homebush for the Olympic infrastructure in the early '90s. An architect business colleague was briefed with removal to Botany of certain business structures. That was the easy part. He advised the governing body of the day that extensive remedial works would be required on the site allocated for new infrastructure at Homebush (costing millions) before the building commenced. Old fill, ground pollution etc. He was in effect told to 'forget it'. Democratic corruption, as such breakdown in both trust and honesty. The breakdown in law and order. No longer, keep the honest, honest and punish the guilty before human nature kicks in and they commence 'justification of action'.

What a sad indictment of a failing society that some smart arse coined the term 'whistle-blower'. Simple freedom of speech, their right to constructively (and I stress constructively) present an opinion of a given situation or practice. Try telling politicians, that with some 700,000 unemployed persons, our total educational/training regime is in crisis and has been so for 30 years. Possibly 40. Trade skills and the appropriate industry shortfall have been evident within the industry for 40 years to my experience. Courses at such institutions as TAFE proved in many instances, totally impractical for a career opportunity.

Certificates that meant nothing, completely ignored by industry recommendation. Degreed and unemployable. Political cancer.

Speaking of cancer, Prof. Gurney increases my tumour reducing medication to the highest dose of 120mg. The symptoms remain the same, the real concern being neck and throat, thyroid and now recurring lung circumstances. Bending down to put Katie's socks and shoes on and it's as though everything switches off for a few seconds, coming up gasping for breath. However, I am still afraid. I feel like a fraud. "Is this really cancer, Professor?"

"Of course, its cancer man, what do you think it is? You just don't present like traditional cancers."

When Henry was dying, he was traditional as it is expected, gaunt, skeletal, grey, and shallow and looks at me, a normal 70 something. I'm blessed. I'm sure that someone has guided my life balance. It's been wonderful, with very few regrets with only one request, that I make it to support Katie to the end. I am not afraid of death, only leaving a planet to young people in such an abysmal mess. Governed by corruption and greed.

We continue our requests, emails, snail mail requesting advice. All communication goes unanswered. I started to realise that my birth certificate is fake. I was actually born on Mars. There is actually nothing wrong with this Martian's computing skill, it's more human distaste for committing to word an answer. Unless it's qualified in a legal term. That's why humans in Public Service authorities or inefficient companies prefer phone calls (often never answered for example Centrelink). The phone call will often confuse you totally and generally never answer the question that you asked in the first place. So, I have concluded that Martians are the decent people (termed on Earth as whistle-blowers), who believe in freedom of speech. A disturbingly disappearing opportunity once more constrained by the power of public office and its minions, the politicians.

(50/50 Rule). How is it that we have been aware of these significant issues to our health for so long? Growing expediential each decade, only to see any real acknowledgement, when the economic reality hits home and it becomes overpowering. Obvious, that if we maintain this excessive dangerous lifestyle, the burden on the taxation structure will be (is) totally unsustainable. This is notwithstanding lower education standards, inappropriate workplace preparatory training. And reduced in house corporative management/workforce training. The inability to create agility/flexibility through the right off-hire or

fire and appalling world standard productivity comparison. In short, we are fat, slow, complacent and demotivated.

Where is our pride? How can we have allowed this once great continent to get to this situation? More importantly, how can we accept it?

My Assist nurse in Queensland in 2015 (she came to our apartment to inject my medication) commented as such when I told her we had been to Ipswich Shopping Centre and I was distressed as to the types of people. Grossly overweight, shovelling doughnuts and other such rubbish into their mouths.

Comment – It's a dreadful area – drugs, domestic violence, 2nd or 3rd generation not working, half of them are feral! What a comment: feral. If a contract, extremely well-qualified nurse, can see this disaster, why not 50 years of politicians? Of course, if you receive a response you will be told about the initiatives that they are introducing. The problem is none of these issues have or are working.

Which brings me to another point: strength of character not to be confused with the strength of talking. The inability to accept that something is not right, getting worse and having undesirable consequences on the individual, community and the international community's perception of Australia. When someone accepts, something is wrong, that the problem needs radical change then, and only then, can something/someone move forward. Australians are notorious for 'thinking we are the greatest nation on earth' whilst at the same time justifying failed action or outcome. We have developed through a great period of perceived prosperity. We have come to expect the McMansion (we now build the largest homes in the world) big boys' toys, regular overseas holidays and all the other wanted 'stuff'. Sadly, bought on credit and debt. The largest per capita in the world and borrowings on home equity with significant loan exposure to fixed or interest only. To support what? A lifestyle of instant gratification or is it actually limited strength of character? That we need to surround ourselves with stuff to promote our ego. The belief that 'stuff' makes us more important, better people and happy.

Happiness and its indications are certainly not created by 'stuff'. Singapore recently rated highly in a world comparison of happiness indicators. They don't have the McMansion suburbs; they don't have gambling on every corner. They consume considerably less medical medication, alcohol and foodstuffs. They don't have an illegal drug trade and they have incomparable criminality. Of course, they have the death penalty. Drug dealers are either dead or plying their agony on our children in Australia. I feel that anyone reading the Striates Times would note from the front-page line-up, it's a firing squad, extremely barbaric and would much better suit euthanasia lethal injection. It has now progressed to hanging – just as barbaric. Hell, we do it to millions of animals every day in the cause of agribusiness, euthanasia that is. So why not for human animals who kill or destroy decency? Our children and particularly our indigenous remote community children would be given a chance of life and opportunity, not despair, heartache and premature death through drugs.

I find that while seeing the ongoing and unresolved plight of others, it places our own symptoms in perspective. We are slowly dying; drug addicts are realistically dead. How can our politicians over 50 years, allow this extermination of a race to proliferate?

I wrote to Abbott some years ago, same subject, succinct and to the point. Please note his response: – ***Appendix 3. Abbott Letter.***

Familiar? "We will keep you safe." The terrorist plot! Maggie Thatcher – the Falkland's, Mnangagwa, Zimbabwe. Howard, Blair or Bush– Iraq, the list is endless. They will keep us safe? If so, why do millions continue to die unnecessarily year in, year out, it's a little like the Smith Family, you know the advertisement? One child in six in Australia living in poverty. If so, then the Smith Family (and others) have clearly misappropriated our donations given the reported declining nature of our children's care needs. Do an audit: 50 years of donations, how many billions and how has it been spent? Clearly, they need a new board of governance given the lack of results and then of course we have the words, "No children shall live in poverty by 2000." Remember that! The lucky country, wealthiest on the planet, just go to the food barn they will feed you.

7) Drugs, Mental Health, Communication and Conclusion. Bureaucracy Killing Democracy

Pablo Escobar. Have you heard of him? Undoubtedly, the worst paranoid drug baron we have ever experienced. Billions and billions of dollars in drugs and laundered money transferred with immunity for many years around the globe. An operational organisation that would parallel the likes of Nestle and Kraft in terms of their structure, planning, marketing and distribution. In Escobar's case, however, unlike a legal entity, everything that he organised was through bribery, cohesion, fear and criminality. Competitive drug corporations would either succumb to his integration/takeover terms or they would be exterminated. Wives, daughters, brothers, mothers, no one was immune. He bullied everyone who stood in his way. Eventually being selected for Parliament, so much was the depth of his illicit drug financed objectives. What has this to do with charities or indeed politicians you ask? Well, of course, this was all conducted under the "knowing eyes" of four pillars of the establishment: The Government and its Public Service regimes, various international charities and the church. The Catholic Church to be precise. Every despicable act of murder, extortion and despair for those affected worldwide by his 'drug selling' was followed by acts of reflection, confession and forgiveness by the church. The confessional became his refuge, admit your sins and God will forgive you, my son and we are truly grateful for your contribution to the new church or hospital building fund. He gave millions. He paid for and supported the National Football Team and they started to win. Paid for everything by the blood of drug money and suffering. His only objective; power and money with forgiveness from God. Pastoral care took on a new meaning with Escobar, it was bought love and care.

How could anyone forgive someone that butchered thousands in cold blood and potentially ruined or ended the lives of millions through the addictive nature of the substances consumed? As his power grew and the quest for more prevailed, further erosion in his moral compassion deviated to manipulation of products. Additives of any nature were added to the raw product, anything that was cheap. Increasing the reality of overdose. All accepted and sanctioned by the very persons that we are supposed to revere. And we wonder why the organisations mentioned are no longer trusted by the mass. Capitalism in its rawest state. We continue to experience the broken trust component in our everyday routine.

Register for what was the local community volunteer organisation and one now finds that you pay for it. You are a registered item, a KPI (Key Performance Indicator), they are now the charity, NGO the provider their total focus to numbers and your subsequent return to their investment.

Katie joined one such local group, previously the community hub, now recently restructured as an assistance program for various care needs for the elderly, specifically with dementia by health service. The overriding public service authority overseeing aged care, ACAT and provider services etc. The 'coal face' people that volunteer for these types of organisations are tremendous individuals in our experience, giving up time to help others less fortunate. However, the structure deems you a financial member. Pay your subscription and you are supported, stop paying or attending for whatever reason and you are soon forgotten. No longer does the priest, pastoral care worker, volunteer or doctor knock on your door. You could be dead and only when the notification was officially given, would the Facebook RIPs flood in, what a wonderful period, loved by everybody. A wonderful individual a loving sister. We see it all now, sadly it means little, and your "caring government" does not give a damn. Sure, you can phone the myriad of services that offer phone counselling, unfortunately, the hand of compassion, the caring eye contact, the time taken to visit, the local priest and his cuppa and biscuit routine no longer a reality. We are losing our soul, compassion and humanness. We treat everyone, everything as an opportunity. A capitalist one at that. Hedonism is no longer an option if we are to survive as a species. We have to 'wean ourselves off consumptive wants' and revisit 'moderate need'. We must re-establish our own independence from government, public authority and materialism.

Until we identify and establish an alternative – capitalism must be harvested for the good of the many, not the few. Reduction in return, shareholder dividend and individual wealth would be a start. If an organisation, efficiently managed *and structured, announces a significant dollar return and percentage over generally accepted returns, is that good? Is it acceptable that organisations then announce job cutbacks of a substantial cost-cutting nature? All robotics aside, does this organisation owe it to the community to create gainful employment? Surely, we need to strike an appropriate balance? Employment, pride, motivation, wellbeing. The community vs. individual power, its subsequent control and excess self-gratification and materialism. Is it right that one of the world's greatest Cod fisheries was all but fished out? Whilst the Cod baron pursued his desire for a larger personal yacht? A 200-metre condominium of decadence on the water incorporating wood-burning fires in the study, stateroom and bedroom. Is it appropriate that a Saudi oil baron would build the world's largest mega-yacht and call it 'Tits two' whilst being greeted, as with other world leaders, regularly by the British Monarch? Is hypocrisy part of the human psyche or have we just succumbed to it? We no longer have Confucius, Michael Angelo's, DaVinci, Pythagoras, Aristotle, Einstein or Marx to name a few. Individuals of great wisdom that formed debate. "What could be'? A deeper meaning of life's opportunities. Long-term vision and creation, passionate about their theory, concept or design, not succumbing to 'the day's argument'.*

Separation of power, now blurred in many autocracies to the functionality of personal gain and hubris. Institutions, past centres of excellence, higher thinking, creativity and challenges have become "factories" for churning out on mass mediocrity. Once scholarly and challenging they have in many instances morphed into public service domains of self-opinion, dependent on funding allocation, HEC's and overseas revenue, pushed through at any cost. Dumbed down autocracies that through their own incapacities of knowledge and wisdom, fear debate and challenge to their own self-imposed superiority. Churning out 'pieces of paper' when the future trending data shows no employment opportunity for that particular subject matter, already oversupplied. Sitting, listening to the conversation to date (50/50 Rule) the reference terms to "when did you get the new barbecue? The plantation shutters look great; did you buy them from Accent? We are thinking of buying some. I see you bought a new car; I like the colour, where did you get it from? Did you get a good deal?" And so, the boredom continues. Mention anything of worthy debate, unless it's social media 'written for the day with little positivity to say' or present popular 'days of our drearies', Survivor, the Block, Neighbours or the proliferation of reality TV. There is nothing to say. "Have you read a good book lately?" Pause button.

"The Second Mountain, the Quest for a Moral life, David Brooks, was quite good. Who is he? Wait, I'll just Google it." Heaven helps us. Boring and I only went to Whinney Banks Boys. Thank You Whinney Banks Boys – for challenging my brain.

Let me just say, I do not see myself as particularly articulate, possibly average in education as to the standards of the '50s and '60s. Nonetheless significantly higher than that taught today. I make no apology, I am the product of my own doing, and I just did not pay enough attention nor study hard enough in those short formative years. I was an idiot.

However, there are two individuals in my life that, whilst they do not realise it, I have great respect for their past scholarly self-discipline and subsequent career abilities. One is my cousin Chris and the other is Michael, my nephew through marriage. If one were to grade them on the world stage of academia, knowledge and skill, I would rate them out of 10. (Chris 8 and Michael 10). On this basis, I would rate myself as a four. If this hypothesis was proven to be correct, what does this say for our future? (50/50 Rule). If we have propagated many in a failed education structure. On my basis of theory rated as one. And, yet again, data over 50 years of debate, inaction has created this situation. Thank heavens for Indian and Chinese scholars that now proffer in our research institutions. Imagine if I had been allowed to abuse my 'teacher'. Told my Master to 'F-off' or hit him, walk out, arrive at 15 years of age on drugs, do subjects I wanted to do. Forget any form of English, Maths or History and choose needlework or Raki. Where would I be now? Would my lack of personal respect, myself and others, have enabled my career? Would I still be married or would my self-centred weak motivational self have deemed that I now live alone? After three, four or five failed relationships, various children were displaced around the country. Justifying why I had so many partners, getting most pregnant subsequently getting the various welfare options available to me. Would I make excuses for my regular heavy drinking, intermittent heroin, and ice or opium addiction? My visits to the RSL wearing my grandfather's war medals as I lose my rental contribution from Centrelink on the Aristocrat gambling machine. Ever believing, through the fog of alcohol and drugs, that one day I would win the big one. Would my visits to the doctor as a result of my lifestyle end in a melange of reactionary overlaid prescription medication? Returning to my new partner of 18 months, lust, lost and never loved and lose my temper, 'slapping her or him' around in a drug-crazed fit of ice rage?

My apologies, it's not a drug problem, it's a politically contrived statistical misrecording of 'mental health'. Well, this is not Middlesbrough 1960 at 7% of the population. This is Australia 2019 and it's 50% (50/50 Rule) or some of the population. Its drug addiction in its rawest form.

The point of my rating score hypothesis is not to denigrate me, not to put Chris or Michael on a pedestal. The point is simply, we are not all the same; we cannot all be great lawyers or academic philosophical thinkers. We cannot all be surgeons, engineers, business CEO's, research scientists, physics professors. If our educational or political organisations have directed our future in that direction quite possibly, that is why they have failed us and their theories. We are not all the same, thank God. If there is someone or possibly something originally atheist now agnostic, I pray a lot. Not to the politically contrived structure of religious entities. Certainly not to the church. Something more profound, something in my personal dreams. My inner self, my values, my beliefs. I am convinced that we are not alone but only death will tell. Yet my 'luck' continues to hold, and of course, one never gives up hope.

A 'dying brain' is a slow death, generally not painful to the individual, simply a fully lit Christmas tree, fifty or sixty years after purchase and regular use. However, the business went into liquidation and the light globes as they failed could not be replaced. Light globes made from amyloid, tangles and plaque have not yet been reinvented. The routine with no acknowledgement is that which hurts the most. No longer intimate discussions, gratitude, attention, participation or togetherness. The glimpses of your soul mate slowly disappearing. You talk more and more, looking for the glimmer, the old spark. Only to realise that within seconds anything said is lost. You keep the routine fastidiously adhering to a planned program or action and activity. Willing that the memory will be retained longer, that no more light globes will fail. You pray, you cry alone to no avail, the globe keeps failing. You prefer to test the respite in the house care system; this one fails your expectation notwithstanding your own standards. 'Home-cooked meals' provided as a point of excellence, regrettably the quality of 'home-cooked meals' depends on the quality of both the cook and ingredients. Its industrial slop – Australia 1970. Old George Stone would have approved. I don't note one piece of fresh fruit in seven days, simply sugar lased shelf stock cartons or cans, overcooked vegetables and regular deliveries of frozen stock. Teeth cleaning forgotten, hearing aid not removed prior to the shower and medication time changed. All are detailed succinctly in 'bullet point format'. One

A4 page, not a great deal to ask. Too busy on the iPhone and I notice the manager never leaving her office, never saying hello, no welcome, thank heavens for reception, the lady was superb. I phone Katie during the evening, confused, "What is the matter?"

"They gave me a little red pill." I phone the sister.

"Hello it's Phil M°Lean," Katie said she was given a little red pill. "Could you please tell me what it was for?"

Pause. "To make her move her bowels, she has not done so for two days." Well, that's the first mistake, don't lie to me.

"Sister, how do you know that Katie has not moved her bowels? (I don't give her time to answer) I was with her both days. All-day and she did move her bowels."

Pause. "I'm sorry Mr M°Lean it was not on the report."

Was it actually not on a report? Was it actually a suppository? Or was as we hear from the Commission findings, a sleeping pill. Knock the old beggars out for the night. Let me get some peace. I, of course, will never know. I took her home early.

There were small issues, however, like any specific tasking procedure, let one item slip and others follow manifesting in the overall standard objectives deteriorating. Older people don't complain, specifically those with dementia who are unable to articulate their concerns. Hence a Royal Commission. More cost and bureaucracy. Detailed letters – no response. **Appendix 4. An Example of Many Letter/Email Requests for Advice – None Replied to.**

The nursing care home is a prime example of the obvious lack as to appropriate induction, ongoing specific training and development budgets, appropriate to the needs of the particular skill set. Creating the appropriate environment of work output, rostered staff requirement to fulfil all tasks to the necessary and applicable standard of care, diet, medical and operational needs. A very simple entity. You have for example 80 beds with an occupancy rating of 95%. Giving a fixed income based on charge, subsidy at the applicable pricing parameter. You then have fixed and variable expenditure to operate your facility producing a specific pre-tax return on investment. If you wish to stretch this envelope by let's say 5%, increasing shareholder, investor or owner return, then you have but two basic options. Put your prices up or reduce your costs and the appropriate standard requirement. It's in a very basic format as simple as that. Unfortunately, greed clouds the equation as in most instances. Lamb is being *replaced with mutton figuratively speaking. However, it's in the heart of one's family that you should find comfort and care, not paid workers. As Aristotle appropriately said, "we are what we repeatedly do, excellence is not an act, but a habit." A conceivable problem if three generations over 50 years have been exposed continually to 'the wrong or inappropriate habit' as opposed to striving for excellence. Regrettably, we have in many instances taken the easier option believing that 'she'll be right', 'no worries' would be classified in Howard's recent terminology as 'good enough'. This once more makes the process of parenting, education, applicable discipline and mentors supremely critical to the stability of the general population.*

A factor of the respite care sector is that in all instances of visitation to various reviewed options (10 or 11) one common factor prevailed, limited activity. This is clearly a combination of age, agility, mental capacity and personal preference. However, the 'sitting in a chair doing nothing, saying nothing, must surely in part hasten the progression of ageing and dementia'?

I fully appreciate the complexity of this individualised problem, not, however, that an answer has not been found of this situation and implemented as a standard of protocol. Maybe it has, just not in those businesses that we visited. We are about 'to test the waters so to speak' shortly in another business care factory. Let's hope it's better than the first one.

More and more Katie would sit quietly, saying nothing. No longer a visit to the library and the newspaper. If 'looked at' invariably results in three or four reviews of the same page. Not aware that she is doing that. Do I know if she actually reads the particular topic? If a particular article is suggested, a subject that had possibly been of interest previously and questions are asked, there is no longer the ability to form the words, even with prompting. My greatest fear, an empty vessel. A dark room, the only light globe left working in the hall. When she will not know me. The beginning suggests the end. Till death do us part. The fact is this; I do not want her to go into a home to see her deteriorate more rapidly than that, which is already occurring. However, the actual circumstances may well dictate that choice for me. My latest report to Prof. Gurney indicates further activity in general symptoms of the carcinoid; more frequent headaches, sore throat and tongue (oesophagus), gasping for breath when bending down. For example, putting socks, shoes on for Katie. Unbelievably weary, yet not tired, nausea and of course, the constant hot flush body heat (almost explosive) thyroid.

This of course the double whammy, dealing with my own internal and physical decline whilst coping with Katie's needs. A dialogue of symptoms increasing, also in severity, has to be asked, often told, to remove tooth plate, clean teeth, swallow daily medication, wash bottom, take down pants prior to the toilet, sit in the chair, not the floor.

These all follow the process that I have adopted as 'show and ask' then 'show and tell' regrettably more and more the actionability lost irrespective of the discussion. This of course results in the eventuality of doing the talk for her.

Last night she did not wish to start eating dinner until 'the others arrived'.

"Who are the others, dear?"

"Err, um! I can't remember, I'll have to get back to you." I'll have to get back to you, now recurring parts of the conversation. However, you never give up. Anyone caring for a person with dementia may experience an extreme slowing of movement, which can be destabilising to the carer. You have to read the sign and compensate accordingly. I find that as Katie sleeps later if I wake her for the toilet around 6:00 am she will not generally wet herself. However, one has to guide her very slowly to the toilet (I stress slowly) and then help her to (A) find the toilet and (B) actually sit on the pan. We have found that the raised disability toilet seats, a 150cm and separate side rail frame help immensely. Specifically, in "finding the seat" as opposed to potential fails in missing the pan. Colour is another predominant factor, if all colour is white, colour breaks are required to determine let's say the white toilet seat from the white tiled floor.

I mentioned earlier my opinion of charities, NGO's and the like. It's a no-go zone. Who would challenge the Catholic Church for their pastoral care? Many did in the 70's refusing the 10% taken from the wage. My uncle was one. The Smith Family, one in six children living in poverty in Australia. How can that be so, given the past 50 years of government funding to different forms of welfare safety nets? The lucky country, the best country on the planet. How can save the children requests $10.00 per month, sponsorship for a child in Asia when adopting a Koala, requests $15.00 per month. Someone will suggest the cost of a living – fair point. However, I see little reality in a bear to a baby. Maybe that's why America coined the term kid. Adopt a tiger, World Life Foundation $15.00 per month. My concern here is not long after my father's charity comment in the 1960s, Ethiopia. We were deluded with the salvation of saving of a species in the '70s.

Lions
Tigers
Elephants
Rhinoceros
Hippopotamus
Monkey

Not long after this, all tax-free regimes. So why have we lost so many species in this period? Why are we now creating embryos to save the last two of the white rhino species? Where has all this money gone?

Let's go back to our caravan park. The daughter of a park employee forms a not-for-profit organisation, they very quickly had a new Tarago; of course, they need that for the dance studio competitions children's transport. All from the administrative allowance. Ho! Yes, and I forgot, guide dog puppies, $10.00 per month. How could anyone deny the blind and beautiful supporting guide dog?

Well, this is my opinion on that which has become the misuse of the original charters of charities.

Firstly, I would suggest one determine the extent of charitable registrations within the last five years, it is thousands.

Again, politicians many years ago, saw the commercial economics of charitable, not for profit organisations. By taking the pressure off the public service departments and their respective budgets.

Countries, such as America, saw the opportunities in the 1950s to set up non-government aid organisations. Supporting their internal production supply chain, agriculture and pharmaceutical being two specifics. This undoubtedly helped business! Balance sheets, in many instances, within organisations that would require protectionism, if to compete on the emerging open market theories. One could also consider the protectionist nature of the Chinese business entities, as they, through Deng slowly captured overseas opportunities by subsidising production costs – electricity, water, gas, building structure etc. All the while Europeans, well into the '90s, were thinking, "Slanty eyed Coolies still waded the rice paddocks with a bullock, not a Massey Ferguson." They did. Chinese workers that is. However, next to the rice paddock were factories. Lots of them. Slowly eroding sales opportunities of international competitors in steel and its many bi-products, textiles, footwear and general household goods. Producing cheap goods for the world's markets, ignored by arrogance.

As American industries struggled (think Japan, think automobiles) they ramped up their aid supply. More so the policeman of the planet. So back to the topic – charity. Over a ten-year period, 90/96 billion US dollars was aided to Ethiopia. The first question and good accounting practice. Where did those goods and services go? And secondly, why is Ethiopia after Nigeria the most corrupted country on the planet? They and others failed. How much has been spent in Afghanistan and what has it actually achieved? Ask Karzi and others to open bank accounts.

I recollect a recent figure of US $960 billion spent on an aide to Afghanistan. A total absolute failure. Creating an industry for the wrong reason, with the wrong outcomes, most importantly ultimately damaging the ethos of the particular country in question. Certainly not achieving peace.

Katie once more goes into respite for two weeks, my praying, considering that which is presently transpiring regards the Royal Commission – Aged Care. Not to mention queries regards Bupa as our private health provider!

Enough has been said regarding home care incidence, consequently, I do not intend to add to that debate. Other than to say this – I was delighted with the attention Katie received. In the main, the staff were excellent. One should however suggest, so they should be. (A) They are not doing 24/7 as a personal carer is. (B) They rotate individual persons, within this instance, 8-hour shifts (C) the facility is extremely well funded by both government and individual contribution for that care.

I will therefore relate my comment to that which is a common failing within Australian business. That is; one of communication. Once again relating back to the '70s. My mentor Tom Tomlinson and my first management briefing/meeting. "Do you have a notebook?"

"Yes."

"Good, could you get it, please? You will need to take notes."

You quickly learn the consistency, clarity and purpose of your notes.

As a group, a team, you have the ability within the briefing to agree or disagree then moving forward with unity, unity of common purpose. You all have the same objectives for the business, and the communication as such to your team is made considerably easier. Whilst each individual is still their own person and will handle the situation differently, the outcomes for the group will be better achieved. A simple exercise that you may have encountered in seminars. Communication seminar that is, if indeed you have been to one?

You will know the outcome:

- *Fifteen persons in the room.*
- *The seminar coordinator writes the following on the whiteboard, turned away from the participants; "The cat was outside and it was pouring with rain. She was scared, so we brought her inside and dried her fur."*
- *The leader then verbally repeats the above to the first person in the room. He or she asks that person to repeat the statement to the next person.*
- *The message is then repeated to the next person, and so forth, till the verbal statement reaches the 15th person.*
- *That person is then asked to write down that which she/he has been told.*

This is written on the whiteboard and this by way of example is what can be the outcome.

"The car was left in the rain so they put it inside, they dried it."

The breakdown in communication, meaning and intent. Maybe this is why we are wallowing in melodrama or why our business ability now fails short on the world stage. Yet again no appropriate training budget. More focus on shareholder return. The upside of this simple little exercise is this. Write the communication down, note the comment, then rewrite and by the time you get to 15, it's generally reasonably, if not completely accurate.

Consequently, in today's mass communication, if you do not follow through on the specifics, if you do not take notes in briefings, you will be hard-pressed to achieve good management outcomes.

Attached brief of specifics for Katie, this was then discussed and advised what the home would do. Sounds great, except that the people doing the actual care had not had Katie's 'individual specific needs communicated'. I discussed it with the care nurse and it was adopted.

You will note the individualised issues specific to her needs:

- Tooth plate removal and teeth cleaning.
- Referral to sleeping in, and its effect if not left to do so.
- Toiletry/incontinence issues. So critical to her hygiene and sanitary habit.

One of the specific reasons for succinct information changeover, in the case of dementia, is routine. That is: maintaining in the respite facility the same process of routine that is practically possible. I would never forgive myself if she became a statistic that we so often hear. Within reason, at home, nursing home, dead within four weeks.

If our communication was consistent, we would no doubt also limit litigation. Sadly, communication has been relegated to 'spoken word', for the very reason, subsequently making the decision more difficult, given the frailty of human nature today, and driven by text, email, limited face-to-face and social media. The third issue – lies. We are drowning in lies. Not made easier by (A) politicians and their 'spin' (a lie), a 'play on words' to justify the outcome, and (B) the legal structure. Plea bargaining, technicalities, the degree of legal expertise afforded and we can 'get the person off the charge', or reduce the sentence. Knowing that the person is guilty. No longer a moral compass, no longer virtue. Just good old-fashioned ego and income. As such, our prisons are full of individuals who possibly should not be there, had the system worked. Whilst others evade punishment, arrogant in that achievement. Further eroding confidence injustice and the reality of telling the truth. Or, at least what you believe to be the truth, and a meaningful recollection of a given situation. As stated previously, a disgrace, that as a cohesive society we have ostracised 'difference of opinion', freedom of speech and termed those individuals – 'a whistleblower'. As such, consequences proliferate, becoming far more difficult to remedy. Just as with Dementia.

Katie continues to decline as more people shun her, not knowing what to say. Her walk is now extremely slow and most importantly faltering. You realise from exposure to respite; many are far worse. It does not any make it any easier. Changing pants 3-4 times a day, using the toilet (no. 2) in the shower. Wiping her bottom and the excrement on her legs, and you will forgive me for wondering, "Why in hell me?" You can 'show and tell' a procedure a million times, and you finally get it through 'your never give up demeanour'. It will not work. This is it; it can only get worse.

Louise visits her mother in respite with her partner and a friend. They stay for approximately three hours on a Saturday. Staying that night locally so they have a little holiday. Louise does not come back at night to see her mother on her own. Nor does she do so again for one hour on a Sunday, only with Jen. I believe it is fear. Fear that she knows she has failed. That is now 21 times seeing her mother since October 2015, and only once having her stay over for one night. Many overseas holidays, yet never visit her mother for three or four days. The sum total of approximately 40 hours in that time. (Average 2 ½ hours) and I was told to stay away whilst she was in town. "It would be good if you weren't there so we can see her in private." Whilst her 'facial friend' profile infers this loving caring daughter to her mother, and I, as this bad argumentative father, am completely to blame for this situation. Your daughter is a liar, one of the herd and I have not spoken to her for four years. As I said before if I am 100% wrong, she is surrounded by and drowning in melodrama, however, we are supposed to be her family! Why not by way of example: "Jen is going to her Mum and Dad's for a few days" or "Jen is going to her daughters for a few days on our days off. Could you drop mum off at Baulkham Hills? I would like to take her to the x y z for a couple of nights." Or. "Take her home, just the two of us." Or "I will pick mum up on Saturday, taking her to Newcastle for a couple of nights." Nothing. Not even this. "Sorry, Dad I did not realise how difficult Dementia issues can be." Of course, it's all too late now; she clearly does not have the strength of character to handle the reality of the circumstances.

Failed. Like politicians and bureaucracy, 50 years (50/50 Rule) of failure. The Westminster System creating an argument, not mediation. Imagine a company with 10% sales or profit decline? How long do you think the board or business owner would accept this failure? If it reached 20% the board would be questioned. Terminated. However, over 50 years' politicians and their bureaucrats have now reached 50% plus and rising. Obesity, alcohol, drugs, over medication, gambling, domestic violence, notwithstanding our home, the planet. Our future lies with youth, intellect, unity, wisdom and business. Kerry Packer said on a number of occasions, "Never take on the government." Consequently, if one looks at history it continually repeats. However, someone must take on Government and that must be the Combined Might of Business. We can no longer accept repression. Repression by any means. Manipulated riot, dumbing down by Twitter, assassination, legal power, being ignored, misinformation, lies, murder – to name a few means of control. Democracy, Dictatorship, Communism, they are all the same, simply a different guise. We are all being controlled and manipulated. We are expendable. Let them get fat, they may die early and save the NHS on the budget requirement. Don't worry about the millions of Indians that may die (and they did). We need the grain for the Western Front. It is extremely sad, as politicians sit afar to see our young men dying for their country in the thousands. What a disgusting theory. Why not these creators of war fight it out amongst themselves? Just them. We lock them up, demanding that until such time they can resolve their issues, they will be kept there. As a species, we evolve. At least we should do. What we see as appropriate at 19 years of age may well be extremely different to that at 39 or 59. To this end, youth must be our future, their energy, drive and passion. However, it must be tempered with intellect and wisdom. Otherwise, they will fail. Power will crush them. They, Governments will treat them like children. They will talk down to them, incidentally as they do to so many others. Looking after their "mates in business" ever the same cry. The economy and jobs. Their future is secured as the planet dies. No planet, no economy. No economy, no jobs. Always too scared to make the change. Intellectually incapable of "reading the signs" or accepting the science. Born to 74 years incapable of comprehending to 7400 years.

Notes from Virginia Wolfe referring John Maynard Keynes: The Economic Consequences of Peace – J.M.K.1919.

"He is disillusioned, he says no more does he believe, that is in the stability of things he likes. Eton is doomed, the governing classes perhaps Cambridge too. These conclusions were forced on him by the dismal and degrading spectacle of the peace conference when men played shamelessly, not for Europe or even England but for their return to parliament at the next election."

Consequently, full circle from pollution to pollution. The answers must lie with youth, in particular Indian and Chinese youth. As the two largest polluters on the planet, and specifically India as the aspirant. They must embrace new and yet not invented technologies, eradication of fossil fuels, deforestation, and all of the associated issues and bi-products. Creating new, forcing out old. Empires that have been built and succeeded have done so in large part to the adaptation, application and change to new technologies. Those empires then subsequently dimming, as they fail to invest and adapt to ever-newer technologies, as other nations do so in later years.

In recent history, the British Empire failing to the USA. Then subsequently the USA to Japan and of course now China. The Tee's and the Thames, once polluted sewage and chemical waste canals created by industrialised capitalism are free-flowing relatively clean rivers. Wildlife and fish re-birthing in the environment. Not so the Nile, Ganges, Mekong or Yangtze. Not to forget the Amazon. There are limited energy-wasting Glass Mountains in Middlesbrough, life is relatively simple. Many are quite frugal and whilst human nature 'takes morE' if available, they cannot 'get it', they accept alternatives. No longer the mass structures of Dorman Long or ICI. Nonetheless, the population lives comfortably. Big is not better. As such, as I have previously stated, if any nationality thinks and acts on: 'it's now our turn and time' utilising present theories of economics or industry, we will not survive.

Can you imagine for one moment and contemplate? If the intellectual capacities (young brilliant creative's) of the United Kingdom and Germany had amalgamated in peace not power in 1932? Can one not see what could have been achieved as a collaborative force of imagination and invention? Von Braun only one, Barnes Wallace another. Imagine if young Indian and Chinese minds came together today, with a targeted objective of 'Earth salvation' that could be achieved? If all nations combined their mindset to curing Cancer, Dementia, Diabetes? Notwithstanding the associated problems of economic theory to capitalism, consumption, scarcity and our home, planet – Earth.

Mensa is the answer, Business and Technology the vehicle and Youth the energy. Bureaucracy must be dismantled, streamlined and coordinated into structures of nimble concise support. Ministers must be forced to report and act on the science, not the ballot. Universities – Harvard, Cambridge, Oxford and Yale must re-establish academia, not administration. Academia must be revisited as a passion, not pensions. 'Me' must be shunned. 'We' must be embraced. We must rectify the cause, not the outcome.

It would be remiss of me if I did not mention:

- *The Legal Profession. Its complication of matters. It must take a serious look at itself, what its objectives now are and that which it aims to*

achieve. If by its confrontational demeanour, it has added to the problem, not the resolution.
- The Media. "No news is bad news." "Good news does not sell." Do we indeed have too much of it? Bad news that is. Negativity abounds. Melodrama prevails and we are drowning in it. News repetition has killed sensitivity. Who cares if little Johnny broke his neck doing 140km on his unlicensed motorbike whilst drunk? His family does and that should be it.

The two industries, Capitalist in totality are intrinsically linked. Defamation, lies, power and control, working the system. Not necessarily solving the cause.

And God. A deeply personal belief in love, good and spirituality and the establishment. The Church, Mosque, Temple or Synagogue. Whatever the terminology. A structure. Hierarchical in all instances. A meeting place of like mind. A refuge, a hub. Conspiracy or confessional.

Whether praying to symbols, sacrificial ceremony or differing theory, it has never caused the rain to fall, stopped deforestation or drugs. It has not stopped sea-level change or warming, volcanic eruption, poverty, flood or famine. It has not stopped addictions or alcohol abuse, gambling, or domestic violence, slavery, child abuse. It has not stopped fiscal debt burden, international monitory manipulation or bankruptcy. It has created many wars. No Captain Marvel or superhero to solve our own created problems through ignorance.

I am not suggesting that we should not have the freedom of choice to believe in someone or something greater than ourselves. Just don't expect that whatever that is, to solve our problems. Only we, as a collective can do that. We created the mess that we now find ourselves in and we have to fix it. Evil presently outweighs good and it must be revered for the sanity of humanity.

Subsequently, we have to keep 'jobs'. We have to keep the system working because we are 'locked-in' to economic theory as it presently stands. Dog eat dog so the problems magnify and manifest. We will continue to create failure (50/50 Rule) soon to become 60/60. Whilst the planet declines at an ever-increasing rate. There has never ever been 'a level playing field' in the present theories of economics. Therefore, in my humble opinion:

Our future, as an intellectual species, must lie with Uncompromised_Change based on non-emotive facts.

And to my theory and conclusion:

Mensa Matters®

An intellect statement of ecology, equality and earth economisation.

A five-year study to be conducted by only the planet outstanding Mensa Minds.

Objective:

To determine a Means by which the human race can all live a fulfilled sustainable lifestyle, considering the scarcity of the resource. Whilst maintaining evolving ecosystems, ensuring those structure(s) established to fulfil all the Means, whilst creating a model for equal decision.

As one ages, philosophical thought may surface, regardless, one thing does come to bear, and we are all accountable for our destiny. Issues that appeared insurmountable in youth, daunting, now a mere memory of insignificance. Why didn't we just do that? So simple if you keep it so. Being honest with yourself and others, standing up to your conscience not blaming the generation before, as we are all equally to blame. No ulterior motive.

Katie and I have been extremely lucky (that word again). We have been exposed to many experiences in life. We have not squandered resources whilst maintaining a comfortable regime. We do not wish for death, nor fear it. Only that which we will leave behind. Bureaucracy killing Democracy.

"When we are capable of timed matter transfer, we may start to understand life, creation and our soul."

Income earned by the author from the sale of this book will be donated to a nominated dementia research facility – not a charity.

Key Words

Mensa
Matter(s)
Ecology
Equality
Economisation
Uncompromised
Sustainable
Fulfilled

Dementia
Public Service
Politician
Incompetence
Incontinence
Trust
Love
Loyalty

Bureaucracy
Indecision
Mediocrity
Melodrama
Waste
Misappropriation

Independent
Dreams
Persistence
Dedication
Greed
Education

Capitalism
Communism
Pollution
Consumption
Democracy

"Bureaucracy Killing Democracy"

Appendix

Appendix 1. Hunt/Deakin Letters

Phil Mclean

From:	Phil Mclean [katie.mc]
Sent:	08 January 2019 08:41
To:	'Mr Greg Hunt.MP Minister for Health.'
Subject:	FW: Deakin University: Assessing Cost-Effectiveness of Obesity Prevention Policies in Australia

From: Phil Mclean [mailto:katie.mc   ]
Sent: 07 January 2019 12:25
To: 'Mr Greg Hunt.MP Minister for Health'
Subject: Deakin University: Assessing Cost-Effectiveness of Obesity Prevention Policies in Australia

Dear Minister,

Could you please advice if you will be submitting to Cabinet, the recommendations outlined in the Obesity Prevention report, for considered legislative change? Regarding the reference to "sugar", I would suggest the term Fructose be included-not to create legal ambiguity. Specifically as this syrup (wet milled corn starch) is generally cheaper than sugar and used in anything that requires the "sweet addictive hit"

In terms of Junk food Advertising I would like to offer a quote that was made some time ago that I believe expresses the problem our children now face.

" The increased availability of food (especially sugary, snack food, or any other) targeted at children, together with an environment in which children are able to effectively 'howl for it ,and in which this pester –power is leveraged by marketers, has led to explosions in children's ill-health. Over US$10 billion a year is spent marketing food to children in the United States alone. According to Richard Watts,Coordinater of the children's Food Campaign at the UK group Sustain, for every dollar spent promoting healthy food globally US$500 is spent on promoting junk food. The kinds of advertising that lead to paediatric disease aren't restricted to print or television. Advertising media, and the needs to which they cater, are woven into the fabric of children's lives, from text books to cyberspace to playgrounds to parks to packaging."

Would the Minister also consider my comments regards the addictive manipulation of food manufacturing/production and by product of excess packaging/food waste?

In terms of the Obesity epidemic (63% of population), its associated unsustainable mental and physical health cost and reduced life expectancy, I would recommend the Minister informally visit (sit and observe) a lower socio economic demographic food court. Appreciating that the statistics now present across all categories, this random sample exercise saddens one to starkly realize what addiction is doing to our population. Continued failure to make the tough call will undoubtedly see my rule @ 60/60 in the next decade

Thank you for your consideration
Yours Sincerely
Phil Mclean.

Quote: Stuffed and Starved- Markets, Power & the Hidden Battle for the World Food System. Raj Patel.(read in 2007-extremly relevant to today with significantly greater negative outcomes and of course positive shareholder returns.)

From: Phil Mclean [mailto:katie.mc@   ]
Sent: 19 December 2018 09:07
To: 'e.snashallwoodhams@deakin.edu.au;
Subject: CONSEQUENCE AND SUCCSESIVE FAILURE OF PUBLIC SERVICE POLICY RECOMMEDATION AS A RESULT OF CONSUMPTIVE DRIVEN ECONOMIC POLITICAL STRATEGY SINCE 1970.

Ref: Assessing Cost-Effectiveness of Obesity Prevention Policies in Australia

Dear Ms Snashall Woodhams,

Over the past 50yrs, and each successive decade, we have seen consistent growth in the following population categories:

- 50% Grossly overweight.
- 50% Oversupplied and dependent on prescription medication.
- 50% Drinking alcohol regularly at dangerous levels of consumption.
- 50% Taking illegal drugs.
- 50% Addicted to various forms of gambling.
- 50% likely to resort to domestic violence.
- 50% Unable to maintain a meaningful and lasting relationship.

I use the 50/50 rule to highlight the significance of the combined issues-appreciating that the data shows higher than 50% in all categories. Compared to 7-8 % in the 60s. Identifying the failure of successive governments over that period to address the statistical reporting and policy recommendations. This is not the profile of a forward thinking, productive and cohesive population. It is certainly not populist. Definitely denial. As a long time retired executive in the branded food industry I would make comment on Obesity, however suggest all categories have causal link. The overriding issue is Keynesian doctrine. He was more philosopher than Economist as opposed to those of today who only understand algorithms. Subsequently, I doubt today if, alive to re-consider his theories, that they would bear little in common to his previous writings. As such Consumption- considering the frailty of human nature and Addiction:

Brand leaders such as Nestle/Kraft (ak Cargill)- manipulated addictive based products, easily prepared and retailed cheaply utilizing:

- Enzymatic Digestion/Chemical Hydrolysis.
- Syrups/Sugars.
- Sodium/Salts.

The leaders in the 19th Century, such as-Henri Nestle, James Kraft, Forrest Mars and George Cadbury built brand on trust and quality. Fast forward to the 1950s and we see the commenced amalgamations and manipulation of product. Now owned by multinational/investment hedge funds. The only objective being brand dominance/shareholder greed, with no consideration to the public's mental/physical health outcomes. As per Tobacco.

With respect to the co-authors: the principle of taxation increase/advertising suggest little that has not been written here and overseas previously-and only goes part way to solving the problem. And, whilst I agree totally with the premise, I would suggest further consideration and research to the following:

- The chain of events starts with the manufacturer/producer of the goods and the associated resulting issues. Whilst in this instance my comment is related to obesity, an obvious spin of is waste. Both packaging and food product.

If all manufacturer/producers (who created the associated problems-in conjunction with brand marketing) were advised that they must stop chemical hydrolysis, reduce syrups, sugars and salts to applicable health levels in carbonated/solid formats, you would solve significant medical and related problems within 15-20 years. The same period of time that the issues came to prominence from the early 70s. We legislated for trans fat and MSG and, that in part had the desired result. The manufacturers would be forced to change the product base. The price of the manufactured/produced brand would have to increase, as a result of the nutritional cost change, and subsequently the retail consumer price would rise. This takes the cheap price equation out of the market place reducing demand.

Schematics, product sales mix-whatever label you place on it, is both the data capture and basis of positioning within the market. At this point brand positioning creates packaging choice and its subsequent waste. The increases as such, and the composition of the product packaging (plastics,wrap,foam,alloy,cardboard etc)has changed dramatically the schematics of the market. I would comment that the footprint/cost of the market would be reduced significantly by reconfiguring and reducing packaging. Once again the manufacturers have to be told to change. Please see notation.

I fully respect your report comment regards "political will" however given the increasing concerns and associated physical and social costs Western nations face. I firmly believe that we must make these radical changes for the good of humanity-appreciating the changes may not be well received by many initially. This is not a discussion of equality, however the timing is now appropriate.
I thank you for your consideration.

Yours Sincerely,

Phil Mclean.

Footnote: As a CMM Coles Myer (1985) on a study tour in both Germany and Japan. The objective: to review Siemens Nixdorf POS/Data capture systems and automated food service logistics.
One issue over and above the purpose of my visitation has stayed profoundly in my mind to this day. Reviewing a range of pre- packaged branded food, tasting the products-Then EATING THE PACKAGING. Of course all I was interested in was increasing sales, margin and profit at that point in life's cycle. In discussing the packaging issue with a friend who worked as a senior executive within the tyre industry. His comment was ".Phil do you really think that Dick Pratt (Visy) would welcome the suggestion of edible packaging". We have bought dozens of patents for tyres that do not wear out-have you ever seen any of the tyres sold? No-for the obvious reasons.

Phil Mclean

From: Minister Hunt [Minister.Hunt@health.gov.au]
Sent: 14 June 2019 10:59
To: Phil Mclean
Subject: Automatic reply: Obesity and packaging [SEC=No Protective Marking]

Thank you for your email. I appreciate that you have taken time to write to me and I will endeavour to get back to you as soon as possible, however, due to the high volume of correspondence I receive on a daily basis, I cannot reply immediately.

If you are a constituent of the Flinders electorate, please feel free to contact my electorate office on (03) 5977 9082 or keep updated on my latest work by visiting www.greghunt.com.au

Regards,

The Hon Greg Hunt MP
Member for Flinders
Minister for Health

Appendix 2. Royal Commission Notation

Phil Mclean

To: The Royal Commission into Aged Care: Commissioners Ms Lynelle Briggs, Mr Richard Tracy
Subject: The progressive road blocks to Aged Care and peace of mind.

Dear Ms Briggs and Mr Tracy,

Appreciating that the terms of reference do not action individual cases, I would be grateful if this submission could be considered under "any matters that the Royal Commission considers necessary ". It is the culmination of frustration trying to navigate a broken system. In our 70s, my wife has Alzheimers, and, until recently I have never had any form of public service welfare, nor my wife- only in her older age. Whilst the submission may appear simplistic I would suggest that our experiences highlight the business failings and subsequent cost to taxpayers without the intended care objectives. The attached is self explanatory:

- Request for email contact to determine (only short format available) suitable respite care providers with Dementia skill set- please see response.
    - Sent request for support to the email response- Myagedcare@dss.fms.gov.au No reply.
    - Resent original with follow up request. No reply.

There is NO excuse that this authority, irrespective of what they think of my questions, did not respond or advice a contact to whom I should email. This issue is far bigger than my request-this is another example of abuse of power, duplicity and inappropriate distribution/use of funding. My Aged Care is a Public Service Authority, funded by taxpayers, to oversee that appropriate outcomes occur within- in this instance: care providers in both the Public and Private sectors of Aged Care. It is not the Government. Regrettably, Ministers are all too often not long enough in a specific portfolio to enable appropriate leadership and cultural change, therefore become merely "puppets" of the Public Service system. As opposed to leading. I am not detailing the myriad of conversations/issues I have had with others in similar circumstances or those that I have dealt with-see notation. However, state that all initial discussions(to enable future respite or aged care) is met with autocracy and red tape. Commencing with GP Care plans, ACAT, Centrelink and the multi tear layers of Bureaucracy and drop down shared income/cost stream operatives.

The outcome being less funding for the physical requirements at the coalface. It is extremely frustrating, insulting and embarrassing to be treated like a child. You cannot respectfully challenge the status quo within the systems, it prompts autocracy and you ultimately achieve nothing. Outwardly paternalistic caring individuals who, in too many instances actually do not give a damn-principally going through the routine. You are purely a statistic-very humbling after 50 years of hard work. Simply the wrong person, for the wrong reason, making the wrong decision.

Having experienced multi-site/large workforce environs I would suggest that,(and, as a result of our past respective senior executive exposure) one would find in many instances: a toxic workplace, controlling mentality, duplicity and inefficient productivity regimes. Consequently spiralling aged/health care costs, and subsequent funding dilution, without the appropriate objective of meaningful care.

As with the Banking Commission-Justice Haynes only articulated what a reasonable person had been aware of for many years. Namely a culture of greed (and power)driven by governing boards intent on increase of shareholder wealth-at the cost to community expectations and obligations. Chief executives, if disapproving of the culture, would have been "shown the door "and subsequently the fragility of human nature prevails. With the relevant Public Service watchdog entities failing to act accordingly.

In basic format within Aged Care, we have too many inefficient organizations, not for profit, charities and care providers- all "jumping onto the gravy train" of an ageing population taxpayer funded Government initiative. Subsequently the lack of integration, accountability and transparency, red tape and "top down" bureaucracy, will ultimately waste $ billions. Not even honouring the "motherhood statements that its (Aged Care) dialogue infers in its marketing blurb ". The later years of dignified care that our ageing population

deserve will defiantly deteriorate further, unless the findings of the commission specifies much needed remedial action-even if it does" open a can of worms" into Public Service inefficiency, which is ultimately failing the private sector and Government.

Yours Sincerely,
Phil and Katie Mclean.

Phil Mclean

To: royal commission-aged care
Subject: Notation : General Comment.

Numerous Think Tanks (inclusive of the Oxford Economic Forum) have recently passed comment on issues within the National Health System –UK.
    The basic premise is that "Back of House" operatives, waste time developing operating method study procedures, flow charts and staff rostering regimes etc. With, in most instances, no consultation with the "Front of House "operatives –who are constantly understaffed and paid less. The suggestion is a ratio of 3 to 1 –back of house/front of house.

The financial structure should be transparent and basically : How many $ are allocated, how much gets to the provider-the difference. Then how much is allocated by the provider for the care,-the difference. You then simply have the misappropriation/inefficiency of funding in basic format.eg:
    Funding = 100%
    Provider = 50 %
    Care   = 25 %   Simply: the cost to facilitate the care is 75% of the original funding. The actual care being 25%.
Very early in my career. State Manager-KFC Sth Aust / Hungry Jacks NSW The transparency/breakdown of all cost centres at the trading statement level ($ %) enabled immediate acknowledgement of who was doing what. K.I.S.S.-Very simple, extremely accountable and profit driven.

We have a poor track record of training and development within Australia, as such, often import overseas expertise. One recent example being Ian Mcload.CEO-Coles Supermarkets: Salary $15ml per annum plus results incentives. Job Done. He moves to Bi Low-USA.As such, with a comparable $ budget, how do you engage suitability in the Public Service Executive band for $500,000 to $600,000-you don't. You get-"Peters Principle".

Statistics over the past 50 years detail consistent(decade by decade) decline in the following. All now show more than 50% of the population. The data is now across all demographics, as opposed to the 1960s when the data was in single digits and specific socio groups:

- Grossly overweight.(Deakin Uni-Dec 2018,Cost effectiveness-Obesity @ 63%)
- Oversupplied and dependent on prescription medication.
- Consuming alcohol at dangerous levels.
- Using illegal drugs regularly.
- Addicted to various forms of gambling.

  These are all reducible and needs to be considered. As it is, this is the lifestyle that Australians have regrettably endorsed. Now costing the Aged Care sector an unsustainable future.

Key Issues of the submission:
- Inefficient use and control of funds.
- Autocracy,redtape and duplicity
- Layered bureaucracy and subsequent dilution of funding at the coalface.
- To many operatives who are Ill-equipped to fulfil the obligations of their brief.
- Operatives-specifically national not for profit organizations, are more focused to fund raising/KPAs- rather than their original charter and measurable outcomes/result.

Phil and Katie Mclean.

Appendix 3. Abbott Letter

PRIME MINISTER

Reference: C14/24186

22 July 2014

Mr Phil McLean

Dear Mr McLean

Thank you for letting me know your views.

I appreciate you taking the time to write to me.

Our democracy rests on the conviction that every individual counts and everyone can have a say on the issues that matter most.

Be assured that the Government is purposefully, methodically and effectively delivering our plan for a strong, prosperous economy and a safe, secure Australia.

Yours sincerely

TONY ABBOTT

Parliament House CANBERRA ACT 2600

Appendix 4. Examples of Many Letter/Email Requests For Advice – Not Replied To

Phil Mclean

From: ACRC Enquiries [ACRCenquiries@royalcommission.gov.au]
Sent: 19 March 2019 18:03
To: katie.mc
Subject: Your submission [SEC=UNCLASSIFIED]
Attachments: image001.jpg

Dear Phil and Katie,

Thank you for your detailed submission which was received by the Royal Commission into Aged Care Quality and Safety on 25 February 2019. The Commissioners, the Hon. Richard Tracey AM RFD QC and Ms Lynelle Briggs AO, have asked me to reply to you on their behalf, and I apologise for the delay in responding to you.

The information provided in your submission will help the Royal Commission with its work and will be used only for the purposes of the Royal Commission. The Commission may contact you in the future if it requires more information or would like to discuss your submission.

We appreciate that your involvement with the Royal Commission may cause you distress, and would encourage you to talk with those close to you, your GP or other health professionals. Also, there are Australian Government funded services available to anyone who is experiencing concern or distress from their experience with sharing their story – contact details for these services are available on the Royal Commission website at https://agedcare.royalcommission.gov.au/support/Pages/default.aspx. Trained operators are also available through the Royal Commission information line for callers that are distressed – phone 1800 960 711 (between 8:00am to 8:00pm AEDT, Monday to Friday except on public holidays - interpreter service also available).

Also, if you haven't already done so, you may wish to subscribe to the Royal Commission's electronic mailing list for updates on its work including public hearings as they are announced -
https://agedcare.royalcommission.gov.au/news/Pages/Mailing-list.aspx.

Thank you again for your submission and contribution to the work of the Royal Commission.

Yours sincerely,

Mark Dowsett
Executive Officer
Office of the Royal Commission into Aged Care Quality and Safety

Royal Commission
into Aged Care Quality and Safety

T | 1800 960 711 between 8:00am-8:00pm AEDT, Monday-Friday except on public holidays

---

If you have received this transmission in error please
notify us immediately by return e-mail and delete all
copies. If this e-mail or any attachments have been sent
to you in error, that error does not constitute waiver
of any confidentiality, privilege or copyright in respect
of information in the e-mail or attachments.

Phil Mclean

From:	Phil Mclean [katie.mc]
Sent:	31 January 2019 07:37
To:	'myagedcare@dss.fms.gov.au'
Subject:	FW: Catherine Mclean- short term nursing home respite Care. activity id 1-59055880095

Good Morning,

    Appreciating a busy schedule I would be grateful if someone could respond to the following. You would note from the ACAT report that I have NETS, and whilst my oncologist (Prof.Gurney)has me on a very expensive new age medication, and extremely lucky, I am none the less keen to settle options for Katie-in case something was to happen to me, ensuring her health and security. Thank you.

    Regards,
    Phil Mclean.

From: Phil Mclean [mailto:katie.mc   ]
Sent: 18 January 2019 11:48
To: 'myagedcare@dss.fms.gov.au'
Subject: Catherine Mclean- short term nursing home respite Care. activity id 1-59055880095

Ref: Mrs Catherine (Katie) M. Mclean.
    Husband-Phil Mclean. Preferred communication: e Katie.mc
Local GP: Joseph Walchili. William St Family Practice. Raymond Terrace,NSW. PH 49873255.
Doctors:Prof.B Owler/Dr P Russell.
Date of birth 12/9/1944-born Scotland arrived Australia 1970.
Medicare:
Bupa:
ACAT:68265727
Initially diagnosed with Alzheimer's Dr Jerome Ipp-Norwest Private.2013.

    Dear Sir or Madam,
    My wife's cognitive capacity(short term retention) and personal hygiene (incontinence/soiling) issues have deteriorated in the past 6 months. As such, I am finding it difficult periodically to deal with the symptoms that this dreadful disease presents. Out of frustration at times, I am not sure I am helping the situation and would like to see if a professional female nurse, regards toilet usage, would help retrain the brain to the normal procedures. We have participated in numerous Dementia workshops and last year Katie participated in community get-togethers in Hawks Nest, operated by the Council/Mid coast Health and this has all been off great value. However, given the reality of the circumstances, I would like to trial short term nursing home stays of respite care- improving our quality of life, giving both of us a break and thereby recharging my batteries so to speak. Consequently, preparing for the time when my wife will need constant professional care and support. From my standpoint, that will be my last resort, and only when I am unable to care for her, as I would prefer her with me as long as I can. Sadly, we have no family that it would be practical to become the primary care person, taking over my role.
    Could you please advise a list of care homes approved for ACAT that have accredited Alzheimer's/Dementia professionals and those closest facility options to Hawks Nest. I thank you for your consideration.
    Yours Sincerely,
    Phil Mclean.

Phil Mclean

To: Department of Health-Hunter New England District
Subject: Home Care Package.

Ms Michele Anderson.
Dear Ms Anderson,
My wife, Catherine was approved for the following: Residential Permanent (1- 28889045922) and Residential Respite (1 – 288899237352) in September 2017.
Could you please advise if Catherine would be eligible for a Home Care package, and as such, would she still retain her Permanent ranking till such time required. Could you also advice how one determines the cost allocated expenditure for services utilized from the overall funding allowance.
I have now emailed and snail mailed My Aged Care 5 times and have had no reply to any of my communication request for the information.
Thank you for your help.

Yours Sincerely,
Phil Mclean.

Phil Mclean

To: department of human services
Subject: My health care expenditure to date.

Department of Human Services
PO Box 7821.
Canberra, ACT. 2610

Ref: Mrs Catherine Mclean
Aged Care ID: AC68265727
Date of Birth: 12/09/1944
Residential Permanent: 1-28889045922
Residential Respite: 1-28889237352

Dear Sir or Madam,
My apologies for contacting you direct. My computing skills have left me unable to navigate the website to determine my requirement and would appreciate if you could forward to the applicable department for response.
- What monies from Catherine's allocation have been paid to the two service providers used todate for respite/care.
- The specific dates of expenditure.
- If annual allocation is not fully expended, does this accumulate for the next year.

She will be going into further respite for 2 weeks in September. I thank you for your help.
Yours Sincerely,
Philip C Mclean.